THE WORLD THAT GROANS

CREATION, CURSE, AND THE HOPE OF REDEMPTION

JAMES J. BURKE

FIREPROOF COMMENTARIES

FIREPROOF
COMMENTARIES

ISBN-13: —979-8-9941637-7-1

All Scripture quotations are taken from the King

James Version of the Bible unless otherwise

indicated.

Printed in the United States of America

fireproofcommentaries.org

Table of Contents

Preface

This book did not grow out of my sermons.

That statement may seem strange coming from a pastor, but it is important. What follows is not a transcript, expansion, or polishing of preached material. It is not a collection of messages adapted for print, nor an attempt to capture the energy of the pulpit on the page. This book was formed earlier than that—before sermons are shaped, before outlines are refined, and before words are chosen for public proclamation.

It emerged from the quieter work that precedes preaching.

Long before a passage is preached, it is wrestled with. Questions are asked that never make it into a sermon. Connections are traced, tested, and sometimes abandoned. Assumptions inherited from tradition are examined against the text itself. In the solitude of study, a pastor must think carefully, slowly, and honestly—not to persuade an audience, but to be persuaded by Scripture.

This book comes from that place.

It represents the thoughts, meditations, and theological wrestling that occur before the pulpit—when no one is listening, when conclusions are not yet tidy, and when the task is not to exhort but to understand. In that sense, this work is an invitation. It invites the reader behind the pulpit, not to observe preaching, but to sit across the desk in my study and think alongside me.

The questions addressed here are not academic curiosities. They arise repeatedly in pastoral life: Why does the world groan? Why does evil persist? Why does creation itself seem fractured? Why does Scripture speak of judgment so freely, yet promise redemption so stubbornly? These are not questions that yield to quick answers, and they cannot be resolved by slogans or sentiment. They demand sustained attention to the biblical story itself.

For that reason, this book resists certain familiar shortcuts. It does not begin with philosophical abstractions about suffering and work backward toward God. It begins where Scripture begins—with creation as God intended it to be—and traces how rebellion, autonomy, and misplaced worship reshape the world over time. The goal is not to soften the hard edges of the biblical account, nor to make it more palatable to modern sensibilities, but to let Scripture set its own categories and speak with its own voice.

This is also why the tone of this book is intentionally measured. It is not written to provoke outrage, to score points, or to participate in cultural disputes. Nor is it written to offer therapeutic reassurance detached from truth. It is written to think carefully, biblically, and reverently about a groaning world—and about the God who has neither abandoned it nor excused it.

Readers looking for quick answers or emotional relief may find this book demanding. Those looking for a faithful, Scripture-shaped framework for understanding creation, curse, judgment, and hope may find it clarifying.

If you read these pages, you are not being invited to listen to a sermon. You are being invited into the work that comes before one—to open the Scriptures, to follow their logic patiently, and to consider what kind of world we inhabit, how it came to be this way, and what God has promised to do about it.

Have a cup of tea, get comfortable, and examine with me what God has to say about why we are where we are, and what He plans to do about it.

James J. Burke

Marinette, Wisconsin

December, 2025

1

Creation, Choice, and the Birth of a Groaning World. (Genesis 1–3)

As a pastor, I am occasionally asked why a loving God would allow the horrible things we encounter in our lives. Sometimes the question rises out of genuine pain—a cry shaped by loss, grief, or confusion. It comes from hospital rooms and gravesides, from marriages unraveling and children suffering, from news stories of natural disasters and personal terrors many of us cannot imagine. In those moments, the question is not abstract. It is personal, heavy, and often whispered rather than argued.

More often, however, the question is asked with a different tone. It is posed less as an invitation to understanding and more as a conclusion already reached. No answer is expected. The question itself is offered as the final, unanswerable argument against God. In that form, it functions not as a request for meaning, but as a verdict: *If God were good, the world would not be this way.*

Both forms of the question deserve to be taken seriously, but Scripture approaches them differently than we often expect. The Bible does not treat the problem of evil as a philosophical puzzle to be solved or an objection to be neutralized. It does not begin with abstract arguments about omnipotence, free will, or suffering. Instead, it treats evil as a reality to be explained, endured, and ultimately redeemed.

And it does so through story.

The Scriptures do not open with a debate about pain; they open with a world that is good, a humanity that is free, and a God who creates not out of necessity, but out of generosity. The roots of the world's groaning are not hidden in mystery or buried beneath layers of speculation. They are placed plainly before us in the opening chapters of Genesis. The Bible invites us to look not first at suffering itself, but at the conditions under which suffering became possible.

At this point, an assumption must be made clear. Any attempt to understand a groaning world must begin with God as God. Scripture does not permit us to redefine Him in order to make the problem of evil more manageable. A god who is not wholly good, righteous, just, loving, and eternally unchanging is not a lesser version of the biblical God; he is no god at all. Human philosophy has often stumbled here, reshaping God in humanity's image so that He might seem more reasonable, more relatable, or less offensive. But a diminished god offers no real hope. If God can be bent by evil, He cannot overcome it. If He must learn, adapt, or evolve, He cannot promise redemption.

Genesis refuses this reduction. It begins not with humanity's pain, but with the unchanging character of the One who made the world and declared it good.

This matters, because many modern attempts to explain evil begin in the wrong place. We start with the brokenness of the world as we now experience it and then reason backward toward God. Genesis does the opposite. It begins with God, with creation as it was intended to be, and only then traces how disorder entered a world that was, by God's own declaration, "very good."

In doing so, Scripture makes a crucial claim: evil is not a flaw in creation, nor a defect in God's design. It is not the result of a cosmic struggle between equal forces, nor the inevitable byproduct of material existence. Evil enters the story not as something created, but as something chosen. It emerges not from limitation in God, but from autonomy in humanity.

Genesis presents a world in which goodness is given freely, authority is entrusted generously, and obedience is invited rather than coerced. The tragedy of the human story is not that God withholds good, but that humanity seeks to define good apart from God. The world begins to groan not because God loses control, but because human beings insist on control of their own.

Understanding this does not make suffering painless. It does not answer every question the heart will ask in moments of grief. But it does reframe the question itself. The issue is not whether God allows evil as an arbitrary test of faith. The deeper issue is how a good God responds when the creatures He has made choose independence over trust, autonomy over obedience, and self-determination over life.

Genesis does not offer a detached explanation of this choice. It shows us its consequences. It tells the story of how freedom, once severed from trust, gives birth to fear; how autonomy fractures relationships; and how rebellion ripples outward until even the ground itself is affected. The groaning of creation is not incidental to human sin—it is bound up with it.

This chapter will trace that beginning. Before we can speak meaningfully about judgment, redemption, or restoration, we must first understand how the world became a place where such things are necessary. Genesis 1–3 does not merely explain that the world groans; it explains why. And in doing so, it prepares us to see that the God who allows the world to groan is also the God who intends to heal it.

A World Spoken into Being

Genesis 1 describes the origin of the universe with striking simplicity. God speaks, and creation responds. Light, land, sea, sky, plants, animals, and heavenly bodies all come into existence by the power of God's word. Again and again, the pattern repeats: God said, and what He spoke came to be. There is no struggle recorded, no rival force resisting His will, no delay or negotiation. Creation does not argue, hesitate, or misunderstand. It responds.

This repeated rhythm is not poetic ornamentation; it is theological declaration. The world is not born out of chaos struggling toward order, nor shaped through conflict between competing powers. It exists because God wills it to exist, and it takes its form from His word. From the very beginning, creation is shown to be responsive rather than resistant. It is governed, not autonomous.

This matters, because Genesis presents a world ordered by speech rather than violence. God does not wrestle the universe into submission. He names, separates, assigns, and blesses. The authority that governs creation is not brute force, but purposeful command. The universe is not indifferent to God's will; it is attuned to it.

When Scripture reaches the creation of humanity, however, the pace noticeably slows. Man is not spoken into existence in the same manner as the rest of creation. Genesis 2:7 tells us that God formed man from the dust of the ground and breathed into his nostrils the breath of life. Here, God does something He does nowhere else. Humanity is shaped by God's hands and animated by life that comes directly from God Himself. This does not mean that humanity shares in God's essence, but it does mean that human life is uniquely received rather than merely commanded into being. Man is thus both earthy and God-given—formed from the soil, yet living only by continual dependence upon the Creator's gift of life.

This unique formation places humanity in a position no other creature occupies. Man belongs fully to the created order, yet he lives by a life he does not generate. He stands at the intersection of heaven's command and earth's response, entrusted with the task of extending God's ordered goodness throughout the world. When humanity later rebels, the consequences do not stop with human relationships alone. They reverberate outward, because the one creature formed from the ground and animated by

God's breath has fractured the bond between the two. This unique act establishes humanity's role within creation. Man is not merely another creature among many. He is God's image-bearer, entrusted with dominion not as an independent ruler, but as a representative. Humanity is called to exercise authority under God's authority, extending His ordered rule throughout the world. Dominion is given, not seized. It is a trust, not a conquest.

Importantly, this calling does not imply that humanity stands above creation in isolation from it. Man is formed from the ground and placed within it. His authority is relational, not detached. He rules from within creation, not over it from afar. This bond will matter deeply later, when humanity's rebellion will reverberate outward and the ground itself will bear the weight of human sin.

Even in this early stage, Genesis quietly prepares us for what is to come. A world that responds obediently to God's word is capable of being affected by the one creature who is given freedom to respond otherwise. Creation does not groan in Genesis 1. It listens. It answers. It flourishes. The groaning comes later—not because creation was flawed from the start, but because its steward chose autonomy over trust.

Not Good: Aloneness, Relationship, and Shared Dominion

Scripture pauses in Genesis 2 to record something unprecedented. For the first time, God declares that something is "not good." Adam stands complete as a creature—alive by God's breath, entrusted with authority, placed within a world of abundance—yet God says he is not meant to stand alone. This declaration does not signal a flaw in creation, but a clarification of purpose. Humanity cannot fully bear God's image in isolation.

The significance of this moment is often missed. The "not good" is not sin, temptation, or rebellion. It is aloneness. Before evil enters the world, Scripture tells us that independence is not God's design for humanity. Dominion, like God's own nature, is meant to be exercised in relationship. Authority without communion would misrepresent the God whose image humanity bears.

God's response to Adam's aloneness is deliberate and instructive. Before providing a companion, God brings the animals to the man to be named. This is not a whimsical parade, nor a search for a suitable helper among the creatures. It is a moment of discernment. As Adam exercises authority by naming the animals, he also discovers something about himself. Among all the living beings brought before him, there is none who corresponds to him. The animals are creatures under his care, not companions fit to share his calling. Adam is related to them as steward, but separated from them by nature.

This moment establishes Adam's unique position within creation. He belongs to the created order, yet he stands apart from it. The parade of creatures clarifies that humanity's aloneness is not merely the absence of company, but the absence of shared humanity. Dominion cannot be exercised rightly without communion, and stewardship cannot be sustained without fellowship.

Only after this separation is made clear does God act. He does not give Adam greater power, broader authority, or deeper knowledge. Instead, He gives him another like him. The woman is not formed from the dust of the ground, but from the man himself. This distinction matters. Adam is drawn from the soil; the woman is drawn from man. Together, they stand as equals in dignity, distinct in personhood, and united in calling—fit to bear God's image and share the work entrusted to them.

"This is now bone of my bones, and flesh of my flesh: she shall be called Woman, because she was taken out of Man." (Genesis 2:23). Adam's exclamation is not merely poetic or romantic. It is theological recognition. At last, there is one who corresponds to him—bone of his bones and flesh of his flesh—fit to share the task of representing God within creation.

With the creation of woman, humanity becomes plural, and the image of God is now expressed not merely in an individual, but in relationship.

This shared humanity establishes the pattern for human life before the Fall. Authority is communal, not solitary. Trust is mutual. Dominion is shared stewardship rather than domination. The woman is described as a "helper fit for him," a phrase that has often been misunderstood. In Scripture, a helper is not a subordinate or assistant, but one who supplies what is lacking. The same word is frequently used of God Himself as the helper of His people. The woman is given not to complete Adam as a deficient creature, but to correspond to him—to stand across from him as his equal, supplying what he cannot be alone.

Together, the man and the woman form a partnership capable of bearing God's image and fulfilling the task entrusted to humanity. Neither rules the other; both rule together under God. Their authority flows from dependence, not dominance.

Scripture then describes them as "both naked, the man and his wife, and not ashamed." This is not a comment about physical exposure so much as moral transparency. Nakedness here signifies openness without fear, vulnerability without threat. They are fully known and unafraid because there is nothing to hide and no reason to hide it. Shame does not yet exist because trust has not yet been broken.

In this world, vulnerability is not dangerous. It is the condition of life as God intended it to be. Humanity was created to live openly before God and one another, secure in trust and unburdened by fear. The tragedy of the Fall is not that nakedness becomes visible, but that it becomes unsafe. This makes the later fracture all the more tragic. Sin will not introduce isolation into a previously individual existence; it will corrupt a world designed for shared life. Fear, blame, and domination will replace trust, unity, and mutual dependence. The first thing declared "not good" will become one of sin's most enduring weapons.

Eden, the Trees, and the Gift of Life

From the good world God creates, He fashions a garden. From a world God described as "very good" (Gen. 1:31), He collected all the best and designed a home for Man. Eden is not the entirety of the earth, but a place within it—a cultivated space where God's provision, beauty, and purpose are concentrated. Adam and the woman are not placed in a barren testing ground, but in abundant paradise. Everything necessary for life and flourishing is already present. The garden is not a trap; it is a gift.

At the center of this garden, God plants two unique trees, each revealing something essential about humanity's relationship to Him. The first is the Tree of Life. Access to it is unrestricted. Immortality is not presented as a reward for obedience or a prize to be earned through effort. From the beginning, everlasting life is God's gift to humanity—freely offered, graciously given.

Yet Scripture never records Adam or the woman eating from this tree. The omission is striking. God's greatest gift stands available, but untouched. The text offers no explanation, no prohibition, no delay imposed by God. The Tree of Life is simply there, quietly present at the center of abundance. From the very beginning, humanity's problem is not that God withholds life, but that His gifts are often ignored.

The second tree, however, is accompanied by a command. God instructs the man not to eat from the Tree of the Knowledge of Good and Evil, warning that death will follow. The name of the tree is significant. It is not merely a tree of evil, nor simply a tree of information. Adam already knows good. He lives in a good world, enjoys unbroken relationship, and walks daily with a good God.

The temptation this tree represents is not wickedness for its own sake, but autonomy—the desire to determine good and evil apart from God. To eat from this tree would be to seek wisdom without dependence, to claim moral authority rather than receive it. God offers humanity a life of goodness without the experience of evil, but He does not enforce it. Love cannot exist without freedom, and freedom cannot exist without alternatives.

In Eden, obedience is not coerced and rebellion is not inevitable. Trust is invited, not demanded. The tragedy that follows does not arise from scarcity, oppression, or ignorance. It arises in the presence of abundance, freedom, and life freely given.

The Serpent, Reframed Desire, and the Cost of Autonomy

The entrance of the serpent into the garden does not come with thunder or spectacle. Genesis introduces him quietly, describing him as more subtle than any other creature the Lord God had made. The danger he represents lies not in force, but in persuasion. He does not deny God's existence, nor does he openly reject God's authority. Instead, he questions God's goodness.

The serpent begins by reframing the command. "Did God really say...?" The question is carefully shaped. God's generous provision is recast as restriction. What had been one prohibition in the midst of abundance is presented as deprivation. Suspicion is introduced where trust had previously reigned.

The woman responds by repeating God's command, but already the ground has shifted. The conversation is no longer about God's gift, but about God's limitation. The serpent presses further, contradicting God's warning and recasting disobedience as enlightenment. The fruit is described as good for food, pleasing to the eyes, and desirable to make one wise. Nothing about it appears overtly evil. The temptation lies not in ugliness, but in appeal.

At the heart of the temptation is the promise of autonomy. "You will be like God, knowing good and evil." This does not mean that humanity lacked moral awareness. Adam and the woman already knew good by living in it. What the serpent offers is the right to define good and evil apart from God—to claim moral authority rather than receive it. The temptation is not to become wicked, but to become independent.

The woman eats. Living in perfection, she deliberately chose to know what life would be like in a world apart from God. She desired to know evil. Adam, who has received the command directly from God and who stands with her, also eats—not in deception, but in deliberate choice. Scripture offers no excuse for his silence. He does not intervene, correct, or appeal to God's word. He chooses loyalty to the creature over obedience to the Creator. In that moment, authority is surrendered, trust is severed, and autonomy is embraced.

Immediately, something breaks. "The eyes of both were opened," but what they see is not wisdom. They become aware of their nakedness and are afraid. The wording is important — not *embarrassed* or *ashamed*, but *afraid*. Vulnerability, once safe, now feels dangerous. Transparency gives way to concealment. The knowledge gained is not enlightenment, but alienation.

The Scripture says they knew they were naked, and sewed fig leaves for themselves. It is hard to imagine it was simply physical nakedness that horrified them so. After all, husbands and wives today are "naked and unashamed". Hebrews 13:4 says "Marriage is honorable among all, and the bed undefiled". Rather, it was a sudden understanding of vulnerability. They understood they had been manipulated and became distrustful. Adam was "afraid because he was naked"; afraid, not embarrassed or ashamed. Sin brings division and distrust into the family, community, and society.

Sin's first fruit is not rebellion, but fear. The man and the woman hide—from one another, from themselves, and from God. The harmony of Eden is replaced by suspicion, and the openness that once defined life now demands covering.

The cost of autonomy is immediate and enduring. In choosing to define good and evil for themselves, humanity does not ascend; it fractures. And the world that had responded gladly to God's word now waits under the weight of a broken steward.

Judgment Laced with Mercy — Curse as Consequence, Not Caprice

God's response to human rebellion is neither frantic nor vindictive. He comes walking in the garden, calling out to the man. The question "Where are you?" is not asked for God's information, but for humanity's exposure. The rupture has already occurred. God's words draw it into the open. This is an invitation to confession and reconciliation.

Fear answers first. The man does not confess rebellion; he confesses fear. The woman does not deny the act; she excuses it. Blame begins to replace responsibility, and accusation replaces trust. Sin's fracture spreads outward—from God, to one another, and soon to creation itself.

God, rather than responding angrily to Adam's sin, sorrowfully allowed Man to face the consequences of his choice. God's justice demands separation from sinful man, but it is important to note that man freely chose this separation. It was to fulfill man's wish to understand evil that God cursed the ground. When God speaks judgment, He does so with precision. Each word corresponds to the role each party played.

The serpent is addressed first, and to him God speaks not only judgment but the first promise of redemption. Enmity will exist between the serpent and the woman, between his offspring and hers. One will come who will crush the serpent's head, even as He is wounded in the process. Hope is announced before repentance is recorded. Redemption is promised before consequences are fully described. Why is the first promise of the victorious seed of woman directed toward the serpent, rather than to Adam or Eve? It seems neither Adam nor Eve yet understood the enormity of the choice they had made.

To the woman, God speaks of pain entering what was once life-giving. To the man, God speaks of the ground. "Cursed is the ground because of you." The wording matters. God does not curse the man. He curses the ground for his sake. The world itself is subjected to futility because the one entrusted with its care has fractured his trust with God. Life will now be marked by resistance rather than response. The soil that once yielded freely will now yield reluctantly.

This is not divine pettiness; it is tragic permission. Humanity demanded autonomy, and God allows humanity to experience life under that demand. It was to fulfill man's wish to understand evil that God cursed the ground. Genesis 3:17 "cursed is the ground for your sake" could be better translated "for your benefit". The attitude is not "You caused this!", but rather, "Since this is what you want...". God has given Adam and Eve what they demanded — the opportunity to see evil in the world. A world governed apart from trust in God is a world where labor is hard, provision uncertain, and death inevitable. The curse describes what life looks like when humanity insists on defining good and evil for itself. *(See Appendix for a fuller discussion).*

Yet even here, mercy persists. God does not abandon humanity to nakedness and shame. He clothes the man and the woman with garments of skin. Blood is shed—not by human hands, but by God's provision. Covering is given where exposure now brings fear. Sacrifice enters the story not as human invention, but as divine mercy.

The man then names his wife—Eve, the mother of all living. The timing is significant. Life is named after death has been announced. Rather than collapsing into despair, humanity steps forward into the broken world with confidence, even defiance. It seems neither Adam nor Eve yet understood the enormity of the choice they had made. Here God is outlining the consequences of their decision, and Adam decides this is the right time to name his wife (Gen. 3:20). It seems they were listening with some anticipation to the adventures of their new life. Michelangelo got it wrong — rather than stumbling broken-hearted from the Garden, Man marched arrogantly into the new world he had caused.

The garden is closed, not because God withholds life arbitrarily, but because immortality in rebellion would freeze evil forever. The Tree of Life is guarded, not lost. God restrains humanity's reach until redemption can come through promise rather than grasping.

A World That Groans — and a Hope That Remains

The world that emerges from Genesis 3 is not suddenly godless, but it is no longer unbroken. Humanity steps into life east of Eden carrying both promise and consequence. The ground resists. Labor exhausts. Death looms. Relationships fracture. Creation itself bears the weight of a steward who has chosen autonomy over trust. From this point forward, the world groans—not in rebellion against God, but under the burden of human sin.

This groaning is not meaningless noise. It is the sound of a world that remembers what it was made for and suffers under what it has become. Creation does not groan because it is evil, but because it has been subjected to futility. The soil still yields, but with thorns. Life still flourishes, but with pain. Humanity still bears God's image, but brokenly.

Yet Genesis does not allow despair to have the final word. Even as exile begins, hope is spoken. God does not erase humanity; He preserves it. He does not abandon creation; He restrains its corruption. The promise given in Eden—the word spoken to the serpent—hangs over every page that follows. One will come. Evil will not have the last word. The groaning will not be endless.

This is why Scripture refuses to treat suffering as evidence of God's absence. The brokenness of the world is not proof that God has failed; it is proof that humanity has rebelled—and that God has chosen not to abandon His creation in response. The God who allowed the world to groan is the same God who entered the groaning world to redeem it.

Genesis 1–3 does not answer every question about suffering, but it answers the most important one. It tells us that evil is not ultimate, pain is not permanent, and groaning is not the end of the story. Creation's ache is a sign not only of loss, but of longing. The world groans because it waits.

The Scriptures will trace this groaning through generations—through violence, flood, cities, and law —until, in the fullness of time, God Himself steps into the dust. The breath once given to Adam will be embodied in the Second Adam. The curse borne by the ground will be carried by Christ. The shame introduced in the garden will be covered, not by skins alone, but by righteousness.

Until that day, the promise remains. God has not forgotten His world, nor abandoned His purpose. The story that begins with a broken garden will end with a restored city. The God who permits the groaning is the God who promises renewal.

As the prophet declares, He will give

"Beauty for ashes,

the oil of joy for mourning,

the garment of praise for the spirit of heaviness;

that they might be called trees of righteousness,

the planting of the LORD,

that He might be glorified."

—*Isaiah 61:3*

The World Made New

2

East of Eden: Autonomy, Worship, and the Architecture of Human Ruin (Genesis 4-6)

Scripture never describes Adam's sin as a "fall," as though humanity merely slipped into disobedience or collapsed under a burden it could not bear. The language of Scripture is more deliberate and more severe. It speaks instead of sin, transgression, and rebellion. Adam did not fail because he was incapable of obedience, nor did he stumble into evil through ignorance or weakness. He rebelled because he chose autonomy. He knew the command. He understood the warning. He was not deceived. As the apostle later observes, "Adam was not deceived, but the woman being deceived was in the transgression" (1 Timothy 2:14). The rebellion in Eden was not an accident of human frailty; it was a conscious rejection of God's righteous rule.

This distinction matters, because the language we use to describe humanity's beginning shapes how we understand everything that follows. To speak of a "fall" can subtly imply misfortune rather than guilt, collapse rather than defiance. It can suggest that humanity became evil by losing its footing, rather than by asserting its will. Scripture allows no such softening. Adam's sin was not a failure of strength, but a refusal of trust. Humanity is not under judgment because it made mistakes, but because it insisted on life apart from God.

What unfolds east of Eden, then, is not the tragic unraveling of morally fragile creatures who are simply trying and failing to do their best. It is the steady outworking of a chosen posture. Autonomy, once embraced, does not remain private, internal, or theoretical. It reshapes worship, redefines responsibility, and reorganizes society. Genesis 4 and 5 show us what life looks like when humanity persists in self-rule—when trust is replaced by self-assertion, when dependence is treated as weakness, and when meaning is pursued apart from God.

Importantly, the movement east of Eden is not a movement away from life itself. Humanity does not step into nothingness. The sun still rises. The ground still yields. Children are born. Work resumes. Worship is offered. Culture begins to form. This is one of the most unsettling features of the biblical account. The post-Eden world does not immediately collapse into chaos or atheism. Instead, it continues—creatively, energetically, and productively—but from a different center.

Genesis 4–5 does not describe a godless world. It describes a self-directed one.

This misdirected continuity is the heart of the tragedy. Humanity continues to do many of the same things it did before rebellion—working, building, creating, worshiping—but now without trust. What was once received as a gift is now pursued as an achievement. What was once grounded in obedience is now driven by self-justification. Autonomy becomes the organizing principle of human life.

The first words spoken after Eden underscore this tension. When Eve gives birth to her first son, she declares, "I have gotten a man from the LORD." In light of the promise spoken in the garden—that the seed of the woman would one day crush the serpent —it is difficult not to hear in her words a trembling expectation that this child might be the one. God has not withdrawn His promise. Life continues. Children are still received as gifts. Redemption is still anticipated.

Yet this hope exists alongside a fractured trust. God is acknowledged, but autonomy has already taken root. Eve's confession names the LORD, but the world her children will inhabit has been reshaped by rebellion. The tragedy that follows is not that humanity abandons God altogether, but that it begins to pursue life, worship, and meaning on its own terms. The story moves forward not into disbelief, but into self-rule.

This is why Scripture presents the early chapters east of Eden with such restraint. Genesis does not rush to judgment or dramatize the spread of evil with spectacle. Instead, it traces a pattern. Autonomy moves from the heart into worship, from worship into culture, from culture into morality, and eventually into violence. What begins as a personal assertion of independence becomes a generational inheritance. Rebellion is not reinvented; it is refined.

Evil, in Scripture, does not first appear as chaos. It appears as order without submission. The first generations east of Eden do not reject structure, creativity, or purpose. They redefine them. Worship becomes self-justifying. Work becomes self-salvific. Culture becomes a substitute for trust. Responsibility becomes negotiable. Violence becomes defensible.

Genesis 4–5 shows us how this happens—not all at once, but step by step. The story that follows is not merely about individual sins or isolated moral failures. It is about the restructuring of human existence around the assumption that life can be lived, meaning secured, and justice defined apart from God. By the time Genesis reaches its chilling verdict—"the earth was filled with violence"—the reader has been prepared to understand why. Judgment does not arrive because God is impatient. It arrives because autonomy has succeeded.

What follows in this chapter is not a catalogue of crimes, but an anatomy of ruin. Cain, his descendants, their worship, their cities, their songs, and their achievements are not presented as aberrations, but as expressions of a world learning to live without trust. East of Eden, humanity does not cease to be religious, creative, or capable. It becomes autonomous—and that is far more dangerous.

Worship East of Eden: Cain and the Rise of Self-Justifying Religion

Genesis 4 opens not with rebellion, but with worship. This detail is easy to overlook, but it is theologically decisive. Cain and Abel are not strangers to God. They do not deny His existence, nor do they refuse to acknowledge His authority. They approach Him. They bring offerings. They act religiously. From the very beginning, Scripture warns us that evil does not eliminate worship; it corrupts it.

This is the first great danger east of Eden. Religion survives the Rebellion.

Cain and Abel bring offerings to the LORD, but Scripture immediately distinguishes between them— not by quantity, spectacle, or sincerity of effort, but by posture. Cain brings "of the fruit of the ground an offering unto the LORD." Abel brings "of the firstlings of his flock and of the fat thereof." The text does not dwell on the mechanics of sacrifice, but it does draw our attention to priority and dependence. Abel brings the first and the best, acknowledging that life and provision come from God. Cain brings the produce of the ground—the result of his labor, shaped by effort, drawn from soil already marked by resistance.

The contrast is not agricultural; it is theological.

Cain approaches God on the basis of what he has done. Abel approaches God on the basis of what God has given. Cain's worship is rooted in achievement; Abel's is rooted in trust. One presents effort. The other presents dependence. One brings the work of his hands. The other brings life received.

This is not a rejection of labor, harvest, or thanksgiving offerings. Scripture will later command offerings from the fruit of the ground and sanctify human work as an act of worship. The issue here is not what is offered, but when and on what basis. Cain offers his labor as the ground of acceptance; Abel offers God's provision as an expression of trust. In biblical worship, service follows redemption—it never completes it.

This distinction is critical, because it reveals how autonomy reshapes religion. Autonomous worship does not necessarily reject God; it redefines the terms of approach. It assumes that human effort can establish standing, that obedience can be replaced by productivity, and that God can be satisfied with what humanity produces apart from trust. Cain does not refuse to worship God; he refuses to worship God as God.

When the LORD does not regard Cain's offering, the rejection is not arbitrary or cruel. It is revelatory. God exposes the heart beneath the act. The issue is not that Cain brought produce rather than livestock, nor that he failed to follow a ritual formula. The issue is that Cain approached God without surrender. His offering assumes entitlement rather than dependence.

Cain's response confirms the diagnosis. He becomes angry—not broken, not repentant, not reflective, but resentful. Autonomy does not interpret correction as mercy; it interprets it as injustice. Cain does not ask why his offering was rejected. He does not turn toward God in humility. He turns inward, nursing grievance. Self-justifying religion cannot tolerate exposure. When confronted, it does not repent; it resists.

God's response is patient, personal, and deeply gracious. He speaks directly to Cain, warning him that sin lies at the door, crouching like a predator. Cain is not abandoned. He is not dismissed. He is invited— yet again—to choose trust over autonomy. The warning is clear: sin desires mastery, but Cain must rule over it. Responsibility is still assumed. Moral agency is still intact.

Autonomy, however, rarely retreats quietly.

Cain refuses repentance, and wounded pride curdles into violence. The progression is devastating but orderly. Religion built on self-justification cannot survive comparison. Abel's faith becomes an unbearable mirror. Cain does not destroy his brother because Abel is wicked, but because Abel is righteous. The presence of true dependence exposes false worship, and autonomy responds not with humility, but with elimination.

The first murder in Scripture is not the result of scarcity, oppression, or desperation. It is the fruit of religious pride.

This matters deeply for understanding the spread of evil. Violence does not erupt because Cain lacks opportunity or provision. It erupts because Cain's religion has failed him. Worship rooted in autonomy cannot absorb correction, cannot endure grace, and cannot coexist with genuine trust. When self-justifying religion is challenged, it does not yield—it lashes out.

Genesis does not present this as an anomaly. It presents it as a pattern.

From this point forward, Scripture will repeatedly show that false worship does not produce peace, but resentment; not humility, but rivalry; not justice, but violence. Religion untethered from dependence becomes combustible. It demands validation, and when validation is withheld, it seeks vindication by force.

Cain's story exposes a truth that echoes throughout human history: it is not the absence of worship that most endangers the world, but corrupted worship. When humanity insists on approaching God on its own terms, religion becomes a tool of self-assertion rather than reconciliation. Worship, designed to orient the creature toward trust, becomes a mechanism for defending autonomy.

East of Eden, worship does not disappear. It becomes dangerous.

Cain's offering is the first recorded attempt to justify oneself before God by effort. It is the beginning of a long tradition. From this moment onward, humanity will build systems—religious, cultural, and moral—that promise life, meaning, and acceptance without surrender. Cain stands at the headwaters of works-based righteousness, where labor replaces trust and productivity substitutes for obedience.

This is why Genesis places Cain immediately after Eden. Before cities are built, before culture flourishes, before violence fills the earth, worship is distorted. The problem is not that humanity stops believing in God. The problem is that humanity seeks to control the terms of belief.

By the time Cain lifts his hand against his brother, the logic of autonomy is already complete. God has been reduced to a recipient rather than a ruler. Worship has been turned into performance. Correction has been interpreted as rejection. Responsibility has been refused. Violence is the final, desperate attempt to preserve self-rule when trust has been exposed as false.

Genesis does not moralize this story with commentary. It simply tells it. But the implications are unmistakable. A world built on self-justifying religion cannot endure. Worship corrupted at the center will inevitably produce ruin at the edges.

Cain is not merely the first murderer. He is the first theologian of autonomy.

Autonomy and Responsibility: "Am I My Brother's Keeper?"

When the LORD confronts Cain after the murder of Abel, the question He asks deliberately echoes Eden. "Where is Abel, thy brother?" Once again, God does not ask for information. He asks for exposure. As in the garden, the question is an invitation—an opening for confession, repentance, and restoration. And as before, autonomy answers not with humility, but with defiance.

"Am I my brother's keeper?"

This is not merely a sarcastic reply or an attempt to evade responsibility. It is a theological statement. In a single sentence, Cain articulates the moral logic of autonomy. He denies obligation. He rejects stewardship. He refuses the idea that his life is bound to the life of another. Cain's question is not ignorance; it is protest. He is not asking whether he is responsible. He is declaring that he should not be.

This moment marks a decisive rupture in human relationships. Humanity was created to exercise dominion together, in trust and mutual responsibility. From the beginning, authority was shared, not isolated. Stewardship was communal, not solitary. To bear God's image was to live in accountable relationship—to God and to one another. Cain's question fractures that design. Responsibility is redefined as intrusion. Relationship becomes optional. Autonomy insists that each man stands alone.

Cain's denial of responsibility is especially revealing in light of his earlier worship. Having rejected dependence on God, he now rejects obligation to his brother. Autonomy never stops with God. Once trust upward is severed, responsibility outward soon follows. A person who will not receive life as a gift will not guard the life of another. Cain's theology produces Cain's ethics.

The language of "keeper" is important. To keep something in Scripture is not merely to possess it, but to guard, tend, and preserve it. Adam was placed in the garden "to dress it and to keep it." Stewardship was humanity's first calling. Cain now rejects that calling explicitly. He will not keep his brother. He will not guard life. He will not accept responsibility for what happens beyond himself. Autonomy, having refused obedience, now refuses care.

God's response exposes the emptiness of Cain's denial. "The voice of thy brother's blood crieth unto me from the ground." Cain cannot escape responsibility by denying it. Moral reality persists even when autonomy rejects it. Abel's blood testifies not only to violence, but to broken stewardship. The ground itself—already affected by Adam's rebellion— now receives human blood. The rupture between humanity and creation deepens as violence stains the soil.

Judgment follows, but even here restraint is evident. Cain is cursed from the ground and condemned to restless wandering, yet God places a mark upon him to prevent vengeance. Violence is punished, but it is also contained. God does not permit unchecked retaliation. Even in judgment, mercy restrains the spread of bloodshed.

Cain's response to this mercy reveals the direction autonomy always takes. Rather than returning to God in repentance, Cain moves further away. He does not learn dependence; he seeks distance. He does not embrace responsibility; he flees it. Autonomy does not repent under consequence—it reorganizes itself to avoid accountability.

This is the moment when evil becomes social. Cain's crime is individual, but his worldview is transmissible. By denying responsibility for his brother, Cain establishes a pattern that will echo through generations. Violence becomes possible wherever responsibility is denied. Exploitation thrives wherever stewardship is rejected. Injustice flourishes wherever autonomy insists that one life owes nothing to another.

Cain's question—"Am I my brother's keeper?"—has been repeated in countless forms throughout history. It appears wherever society fractures into isolated individuals, where care is reduced to sentiment rather than obligation, and where power is exercised without accountability. It is the logic beneath neglect, oppression, and indifference. Cain's words are not primitive; they are perennial.

Genesis does not present this exchange as a philosophical debate. It presents it as revelation. Humanity east of Eden is not merely sinful; it is increasingly unlivable. When worship is corrupted and responsibility denied, violence is no longer shocking— it becomes inevitable. A world in which no one is his brother's keeper is a world that cannot sustain life.

This is why Scripture does not treat responsibility as an optional virtue. It is woven into creation itself. To bear God's image is to guard life. To reject that calling is to invite ruin. Cain's defiance is not merely personal rebellion; it is the rejection of humanity's created role.

From this point forward, the story accelerates. Cain's denial of responsibility will give rise to structures that reinforce isolation and control. If no one is my keeper, I must protect myself. If I owe nothing, I must secure everything. Autonomy, having rejected trust and responsibility, now seeks safety through permanence, walls, and power.

Cain will go east. And he will build.

Building Instead of Belonging: Cities as a Substitute for Trust

Cain's next recorded act is striking in both its simplicity and its defiance. After leaving the presence of the LORD, Cain builds a city. Scripture records no repentance, no prayer, no return—only construction.

This detail is not incidental. Cain was told that he would be "a fugitive and a vagabond in the earth." The city is his refusal. It is an architectural response to divine judgment. Walls replace trust. Permanence replaces dependence. What Cain cannot secure through obedience, he attempts to secure through structure.

Genesis does not condemn the city merely for existing. The problem is not development, organization, or human ingenuity. The problem is why the city is built. Cain does not build as an act of stewardship under God; he builds as an act of resistance against God's declared order. The city is not presented as neutral shelter—it is presented as a strategy. In a world not yet scarred by violent climate or scarcity, the rise of fortified, permanent cities cannot be explained by environment alone. Cain's architecture answers not the hostility of nature, but the anxiety of autonomy. Cain constructs stability in a world God has declared unstable. He answers divine restraint with human control.

The naming of the city exposes the heart behind it. Cain names the city after his son, Enoch. The city is not dedicated to God, nor does it commemorate divine mercy. It secures legacy through lineage and labor rather than covenant. Meaning is anchored in human continuity rather than divine promise. The city becomes a monument to self-determination—a place where identity, security, and future are grounded in human effort rather than trust.

This marks a critical shift in the biblical narrative. Humanity has moved beyond isolated acts of rebellion into designed environments that reinforce autonomy. Cain's city is the first attempt to make Eden unnecessary. It is humanity's first effort to create safety without obedience, permanence without promise, and belonging without God.

Cities, in Scripture, are never merely geographic. They are moral spaces. They shape how people live, relate, worship, and understand themselves. Cain's city does not simply house autonomy; it institutionalizes it. What was once a personal refusal of trust is now embedded into stone, culture, and social order. Autonomy becomes durable.

This is why Genesis places the city immediately after Cain's denial of responsibility. When belonging is rejected, building takes its place. If I am not my brother's keeper, I must protect myself. If no one owes me care, I must secure my own future. The city becomes a substitute for relationship—a controlled environment designed to minimize dependence and maximize predictability.

But predictability is not peace.

The city promises safety, but it cannot heal the rupture beneath it. It can restrain chaos, but it cannot restore trust. Walls can protect bodies, but they cannot reconcile hearts. Cain's city stabilizes life outwardly while leaving it fractured inwardly. This is the paradox Genesis introduces early and will return to often: human systems can manage the effects of sin without curing its cause.

Importantly, Scripture does not suggest that Cain's city immediately produces overt wickedness. That comes later. At first, the city simply works. It allows life to continue. Families grow. Skills develop. Culture forms. This is what makes it dangerous. The city does not appear as rebellion at first glance; it appears as success. Autonomy does not announce itself with chaos—it presents itself with competence.

Yet the foundation is already compromised. The city is built by a man who has rejected responsibility, fled accountability, and refused repentance. It is shaped by a worldview that treats trust as weakness and dependence as liability. From such soil, injustice will inevitably grow.

Genesis wants the reader to see that structural sin precedes spectacular sin. Long before the earth is "filled with violence," it is filled with systems designed to function apart from God. Cain's city is the seedbed of a world that will later become unlivable. Violence does not erupt suddenly; it is cultivated quietly.

This pattern will repeat throughout Scripture. Cities will rise as centers of power, culture, and security. Some will become places of refuge and redemption. Others will become engines of pride and domination. The difference will never be architecture alone. It will always be allegiance. Cities built in trust can become instruments of blessing. Cities built in autonomy become monuments to fear.

Cain's city belongs to the latter. It is not the answer to violence; it is the environment in which violence will later be justified, normalized, and celebrated. Autonomy has now found a home.

Genesis does not linger on the city's details. It does not describe walls, gates, or streets. Those details do not matter yet. What matters is the posture behind the project. Humanity has begun to shape the world not as steward under God, but as master apart from Him. The earth is no longer treated as a trust to be cared for, but as a resource to be controlled.

From this point on, evil will accelerate not only through individual choices, but through inherited systems. Children will be born into environments already bent toward autonomy. Culture will form without repentance. Power will concentrate without accountability. The city will do what Cain's question began: it will make responsibility optional.

Cain builds instead of belonging. And in doing so, he teaches humanity a dangerous lesson—that life can be stabilized without trust, secured without obedience, and preserved without God.

Genesis will soon show us the cost of that lesson.

Progress Without Repentance: Culture Untethered from God

Genesis then records a surge of human achievement. Cain's descendants cultivate livestock, develop musical instruments, and forge tools from bronze and iron. Humanity learns to shape the world with increasing precision and power. Work becomes specialized. Skill accumulates. Culture emerges.

Scripture does not condemn these developments. On the contrary, they testify to the persistence of the image of God. Creativity remains. Intelligence remains. Capacity remains. The curse has not erased humanity's ability to build, innovate, or organize. The ground resists, but it still yields. The human mind still imagines. The human hand still fashions.

What is absent is not ability, but obedience.

Genesis carefully withholds something the modern reader expects: there is no recorded prayer, no confession, no return. Culture advances, but worship does not deepen. Work multiplies, and, apart from submissive worship, begins to sustain the illusion that life can flourish without God. Humanity grows more capable without growing more dependent. Progress unfolds without reconciliation.

This silence is not accidental. Scripture is making a theological claim.

Human civilization cannot function without submission. When humanity refuses obedience to God, it does not become free—it becomes subject to power, passion, or fear.

This is one of the Bible's most unsettling truths. A society can become technologically sophisticated while becoming morally hollow. Skill can expand while conscience contracts. Innovation can accelerate while responsibility erodes. The curse does not eliminate human potential; it redirects it. Autonomy does not destroy culture—it repurposes it.

East of Eden, culture becomes a substitute for trust.

Work, once received as stewardship under God, begins to function as self-salvation. Mastery replaces gratitude. Productivity replaces obedience. The earth is no longer cultivated as a gift, but exploited as a resource. Humanity no longer works with creation under God, but works upon creation in pursuit of control.

Autonomy now moves beyond the individual and embeds itself in systems. Tools are no longer merely instruments of provision; they become instruments of power. Music is no longer merely expression; it becomes formation. Technology is no longer merely skill; it becomes leverage. Culture begins to shape what humanity celebrates, tolerates, and ultimately justifies.

And still, there is no repentance.

Genesis is deliberately tracing a world that continues to function while slowly losing its soul. This is not chaos. This is order—an order built on the assumption that life can be sustained apart from God. The tragedy is not that humanity fails to flourish; it is that humanity appears to flourish without returning.

This is why the text moves so naturally from achievement to violence. Progress untethered from repentance does not neutralize sin; it institutionalizes it. When trust is removed, power must take its place. When accountability disappears, dominance fills the vacuum. When dependence is rejected, self-preservation becomes supreme.

By the time Scripture introduces Lamech, the logic has matured. Cain sinned and feared. Lamech sins and sings. Violence is no longer concealed; it is celebrated. Culture, once neutral, now becomes a vehicle for moral inversion. Murder is not lamented; it is memorialized. Vengeance is not restrained; it is amplified.

Lamech's song is not merely a personal boast—it is the first recorded manifesto of autonomous humanity. He does not deny God's word concerning Cain; he repurposes it. Mercy becomes entitlement. Protection becomes escalation. Theology is no longer rejected—it is weaponized.

Here autonomy finds its voice.

With Lamech, human culture crosses a threshold. Evil no longer hides. It explains itself. It justifies itself. It sings itself into permanence. The problem is no longer merely what humanity does, but what humanity now calls good.

Genesis has led us here deliberately. The reader is meant to see that judgment does not arrive because humanity is ignorant, weak, or undeveloped. It arrives because humanity has become capable, confident, and unrepentant. Autonomy has succeeded.

Progress without repentance does not restrain evil; it accelerates it.

Lamech: When Autonomy Finds Its Voice

Lamech marks a decisive turning point in the Genesis narrative.

Cain sinned and feared.

Lamech sins and sings.

The difference is not merely one of degree, but of posture. Cain murders his brother and recoils beneath the weight of his own act. He is afraid, defensive, and restless. Lamech, by contrast, displays no fear at all. Violence no longer drives him into hiding; it drives him into expression. What Cain commits in secrecy, Lamech proclaims in song.

Genesis records Lamech's words with unsettling brevity:

> *"I have slain a man to my wounding, and a young man to my hurt.*
>
> *If Cain shall be avenged sevenfold, truly Lamech seventy and sevenfold."*

This is not confession. It is celebration.

Murder is not lamented; it is memorialized.

Lamech does not deny God's earlier word concerning Cain; he appropriates it. God's restraint toward Cain was given to limit violence—to prevent its spread through unchecked vengeance. Lamech takes that merciful restraint and turns it into a doctrine of escalation. Protection becomes entitlement. Mercy becomes license. What God intended as a boundary, Lamech recasts as justification.

This is not unbelief. It is theological distortion.

Lamech does not reject God's word; he weaponizes it. He does not deny accountability; he reframes it. In his mouth, divine patience is no longer a call to repentance but a guarantee of immunity. Violence is no longer tragic; it is rational. Power is no longer restrained; it is righteous.

Here autonomy finds its voice.

With Lamech, human culture crosses a threshold. Evil no longer hides behind fear or excuse. It explains itself. It justifies itself. It sings itself into permanence. Violence becomes identity, and cruelty becomes legacy. What began as an act now becomes a worldview.

This is the moment Scripture wants us to feel the danger of progress without obedience. Lamech stands at the intersection of cultural achievement and moral inversion. He inherits tools, music, and social structure—and uses them not to restore trust, but to celebrate dominance. Culture no longer merely accommodates autonomy; it amplifies it.

Lamech is not merely more violent than Cain. He is morally inverted. He looks upon autonomous humanity and declares it good.

In Cain, rebellion still trembles beneath consequence. In Lamech, rebellion has found confidence. Shame has evaporated. Fear has been replaced with bravado. Violence is no longer a breakdown of order; it is the order.

Genesis does not editorialize this moment. It does not pause to condemn Lamech with commentary or explanation. It simply lets him speak. And that silence is itself an indictment. When autonomy no longer fears exposure, judgment is no longer far behind.

By the time Scripture will later declare that "the earth was filled with violence," the reader has already seen why. Violence did not erupt suddenly. It was cultivated. It was justified. It was sung.

Autonomy has succeeded. And the world can no longer bear the weight.

Scripture does not pause to argue with Lamech. It simply turns the page. And on that page, two paths come into view—one that sings of strength and vengeance, and another that does something far quieter: it calls upon the name of the LORD.

Two Lines, Two Futures: Calling on the Name of the Lord

Against the rising noise of violence and self-assertion, Genesis introduces another line. It does so without drama, explanation, or flourish. There is no city built, no song composed, no boast recorded. Instead, Scripture offers a single, understated sentence:

> *"Then began men to call upon the name of the LORD."*

The contrast could not be sharper.

One line builds, boasts, and dominates. The other prays.

Genesis does not present this second line as morally flawless or culturally impressive. It records no achievements, no innovations, no monuments. What distinguishes it is not productivity, but posture. Where Cain's descendants organize life around control and permanence, Seth's descendants organize life around dependence. They do not secure their future through walls or weapons; they appeal to the LORD.

This is not a return to Eden, nor is it a restoration of innocence. Humanity east of Eden remains fallen, labor remains difficult, and death remains inevitable. What has changed is not the environment, but the direction of trust. Calling upon the name of the LORD is not an escape from the groaning world; it is a way of inhabiting it without surrendering to autonomy.

The phrase itself is theologically dense. To call upon the name of the LORD is not merely to acknowledge God's existence, nor to invoke Him in moments of crisis. It is to appeal to His character, to submit to His authority, and to depend upon His mercy. It is worship marked by humility rather than self-justification. Where Cain's offering sought acceptance through effort, this line seeks life through surrender.

Importantly, Genesis does not portray this line as dominant or triumphant. It exists alongside the rising power of autonomous culture, not above it. While one lineage accumulates strength and influence, the other remains largely hidden. Yet Scripture places its weight decisively here. Progress, power, and permanence are not the measures that determine the future of the world. Dependence is.

This quiet divergence establishes the true fault line of human history. Humanity is no longer divided primarily by ability, intelligence, or success, but by worship. One future is shaped by self-rule, the other by submission. One seeks security through control, the other through trust. One organizes life to avoid dependence, the other embraces it.

Genesis offers no illusion that these paths will peacefully coexist. As autonomous culture expands, violence accelerates. As dependence persists, it does so under pressure, often overshadowed and threatened. Calling upon the name of the LORD does not halt the spread of corruption, nor does it reverse the damage already done. But it preserves a line through which God's purposes will continue.

This is why Genesis records this moment before describing the Flood. Judgment does not arrive because every individual is equally corrupt, but because the direction of the world has been set. Autonomy has become normative. Violence has been justified. Power has replaced obedience as the organizing principle of society.

Yet God has not been driven from His world.

Even as the earth moves toward collapse, a line remains—quiet, dependent, and calling upon the LORD. The groaning world is not without witness. Trust has not vanished. Submission has not disappeared. God's purposes have not been extinguished.

The future of humanity will not be decided by the strength of cities or the reach of culture, but by this dividing line. One path leads toward domination and decay. The other, though fragile and often obscured, leads toward preservation and promise.

Genesis has now shown us the cause. The consequences are coming.

The World Poised on the Brink

By the end of Genesis 5, the pattern is complete.

Worship has been corrupted. Responsibility has been denied. Culture has advanced without repentance, and violence has moved from tragic act to celebrated identity. Humanity has not descended into chaos; it has reorganized itself around autonomy. The world continues to function—but on borrowed time.

This is what makes the biblical account so unsettling. The earth does not appear broken beyond use. Families grow. Work continues. Cities stand. Music is sung. Tools are forged. Life, on the surface, goes on.

But beneath that continuity, something essential has been lost.

The question is no longer whether humanity is capable, creative, or productive. Genesis has answered that decisively. The question is whether humanity remains governable under God. And the answer, increasingly, is no.

Autonomy has not merely been chosen; it has been normalized. Worship is no longer oriented toward trust, but toward justification. Responsibility is no longer assumed, but rejected. Power is no longer restrained, but celebrated. Violence is no longer feared, but defended.

The world has not stopped believing in God. It has learned to live without submitting to Him.

This is the condition Scripture presents just before the Flood. Not a world ignorant of God, but a world resistant to Him. Not a world lacking order, but a world ordered around self-rule. Not a world collapsing into disorder, but a world stabilizing injustice.

By this point, the dividing line has been drawn. One line continues to build, dominate, and define good by strength. The other quietly calls upon the name of the LORD. But the balance of the world no longer rests with those who pray. Autonomy has become the organizing principle of society.

Genesis does not yet pronounce judgment here. It simply lets the evidence stand.

The reader is meant to feel the weight of inevitability. A world that refuses submission cannot sustain justice. A culture that celebrates violence cannot preserve life. A civilization that treats autonomy as virtue cannot remain humane.

The earth is still full—but it is filling with something deadly.

By the time Scripture will later declare that "the earth was filled with violence," the verdict will not feel sudden. It will feel earned. The Flood will not arrive as divine overreaction, but as moral necessity.

Genesis has shown us the cause.

The consequences are now unavoidable.

"And God Saw": Divine Grief and Moral Reckoning

Genesis 6 marks a decisive shift in the biblical narrative. For several chapters, Scripture has traced the spread of autonomy through human choices, worship, culture, and violence. Now the perspective changes. The story pauses—not to record another human act, but to reveal divine evaluation.

"And GOD saw that the wickedness of man was great in the earth, and that every imagination of the thoughts of his heart was only evil continually."

The language is deliberate and unsettling. This is not a sudden discovery, nor a reactive outburst. The phrase "And God saw" echoes the repeated refrain of Genesis 1, where God looked upon His creation and declared it good. The same God who once surveyed the world with delight now surveys it with sorrow. The shift is not in God's character, but in the condition of the world before Him.

This seeing is not passive observation. It is moral assessment. God evaluates the direction humanity has taken and names it truthfully. Wickedness is no longer sporadic or restrained. It is great. Corruption is no longer occasional or external. It has settled into the inner life of humanity. The problem is not merely what people do, but what they desire. Thought itself has become bent. Imagination has been redirected away from trust and toward self-rule.

Genesis is careful in its wording. It does not say that humanity lacks goodness in any absolute sense. People still create, build, form families, and shape culture. But the orientation of the heart has become fixed. Autonomy has ceased to be contested and has become habitual. The world is now organized around a refusal of submission.

It is here that Scripture introduces one of its most misunderstood statements:

"And it repented the LORD that he had made man on the earth, and it grieved him at his heart."

This verse does not suggest that God has miscalculated or lost control. Scripture does not present divine repentance as uncertainty about the future, but as a moral response to the present. God is not surprised by human rebellion, nor does He regret creation as a mistake. He grieves because a relationship has been violated. The sorrow of God is not weakness; it is fidelity. Only a God who truly loves His creation can be grieved by what it has become.

Divine grief is the cost of divine faithfulness.

God's sorrow does not arise because humanity has become difficult to manage, but because humanity has become unwilling to be governed. The grief of Genesis 6 is not sentimental emotion; it is the measured response of a righteous God to a world that has exhausted mercy without embracing repentance. God does not grieve because He has failed. He grieves because humanity has succeeded in rejecting Him.

Yet even here, judgment does not rush ahead of patience. Scripture records deliberation, not impulse. God names the condition of the world, weighs it, and speaks of resolve. The language of judgment is sober, restrained, and proportionate. Humanity will be addressed according to what it has become.

This moment marks the limit of forbearance.

For generations, autonomy has been allowed to run its course. Worship has been distorted. Responsibility has been denied. Violence has been normalized. Cities have risen. Culture has flourished. Yet repentance has not followed. God's patience has not produced humility; it has been repurposed as license. Mercy, when continually refused, does not remain neutral. It gives way to reckoning.

Judgment, in Genesis, is never arbitrary. It is the consequence of a world that has made itself unlivable. A civilization built on domination cannot preserve life. A culture that celebrates violence cannot sustain justice. A humanity that refuses submission cannot bear the weight of freedom. What God now prepares to do is not an interruption of goodness, but the restraint of corruption.

And yet—remarkably—the text does not end with condemnation.

> *"But Noah found grace in the eyes of the LORD."*

This sentence stands as a quiet interruption in an otherwise devastating assessment. Grace appears not as reward, but as a gift. Noah is not introduced as flawless or exceptional by comparison. He is introduced as one who stands in a different posture before God. Before obedience is described, grace is given. Before judgment unfolds, mercy is named.

This matters. Grace is not humanity's achievement under pressure; it is God's initiative in judgment. Noah does not halt the coming flood, but he becomes the means by which creation will be preserved through it. The same God who sees corruption also sees faithfulness. The same God who judges the world also commits to its future.

Genesis 6 does not present the Flood as divine rage unleashed, but as moral reckoning restrained by grace. God does not abandon His world; He acts to preserve it—even when preservation requires judgment.

The story has now reached its turning point. The world has been weighed and found wanting. Autonomy has run its course. Violence has filled the earth. And yet grace remains.

What follows will not be the end of the world, but its severe mercy.

The World Made New

3

The Great Reset of Grace (Genesis 6–9)

Genesis 6 does not introduce a sudden collapse of human morality. It records the completion of a trajectory that began in Eden and unfolded steadily east of the garden. By the time Scripture reaches this point, rebellion has matured, autonomy has normalized, and violence has become structural rather than incidental. The Flood does not interrupt the story; it resolves a direction already chosen.

The text is deliberate in its diagnosis:

> *"And GOD saw that the wickedness of man was great in the earth, and that every imagination of the thoughts of his heart was only evil continually" (Gen. 6:5).*

This is not the language of occasional failure or moral weakness. It is not describing isolated acts of cruelty scattered among otherwise faithful lives. Scripture reaches beneath behavior to mechanism. The problem is not merely what humanity does, but how humanity now imagines and wills.

The imagination is the faculty by which humanity conceives possibilities. It is the workshop of intention, the place where actions are first envisioned before they are enacted. Imagination does not compel behavior; it supplies options. It presents images of what could be done, what might be justified, what seems advantageous. In itself, imagination is morally neutral. God gave humanity the capacity to imagine in order to create, steward, and extend His ordered goodness throughout the world.

But imagination untethered from trust becomes dangerous.

As autonomy deepens, imagination begins to generate alternatives to obedience. It reframes boundaries as obstacles and restraint as weakness. Over time, it does not merely imagine isolated acts of evil; it constructs narratives in which evil appears reasonable, necessary, or even virtuous. Violence becomes thinkable before it becomes actionable. Domination is justified before it is enacted.

Yet imagination alone does not determine direction. Scripture locates responsibility more deeply—in the heart.

In biblical thought, the heart is not merely the seat of emotion. It is the center of will, the faculty that prioritizes, chooses, and commits. The heart is where imagined possibilities are weighed and ranked. It decides what is desirable, what is acceptable, and what is worth pursuing at cost to others. If imagination supplies options, the heart establishes values.

Genesis 6 tells us that this ordering center has become corrupted. As imagination offered an expanding range of evil possibilities, the heart began to prefer them. Violence was no longer resisted as a tragic necessity; it was selected as a strategy. Domination was no longer lamented as failure; it was embraced as virtue. The problem was not ignorance, but appetite. Humanity did not lose its moral awareness; it redirected it toward power.

This is why Scripture emphasizes that evil was continual. The heart no longer hesitates. It no longer deliberates between trust and autonomy. The choice has already been made. When imagination presents violence as an option, the heart recognizes it as priority. When domination appears possible, it is chosen. The inner life of humanity has become aligned with destruction.

What makes this assessment particularly unsettling is what Genesis does not portray. The earth is not described as ignorant of God. Worship still exists. Families continue. Culture advances. The world has not collapsed into chaos or disbelief. Humanity has not rejected structure; it has reorganized structure around self-rule. The problem is not disorder, but order without submission.

A world that lacks order is visibly broken. A world ordered around autonomy can appear functional, even impressive. Genesis presents us with the latter. Humanity has learned to live, build, worship, and govern itself without reference to God's authority. Autonomy has not failed; it has succeeded.

At its core, autonomy functions as a form of worship. When the self becomes the highest authority, it assumes the place once reserved for God. Value is no longer received; it is assigned. Worth is no longer inherent; it is conditional. Other persons are no longer encountered as image-bearers to be honored, but as variables to be managed. Their value is measured by proximity to one's desires, comfort, or goals. When self is god, other life matters only insofar as it serves the self's purposes or avoids the self's inconvenience. Violence, then, is not a breakdown of morality but its reordering. Domination becomes reasonable.

Elimination becomes thinkable. What cannot be controlled is eventually treated as expendable.

It is at this point that Scripture introduces one of its most misunderstood statements:

"And it repented the LORD that he had made man on the earth, and it grieved him at his heart" (Gen. 6:6).

This is not divine miscalculation. Scripture does not portray God as surprised by human rebellion or ignorant of its trajectory. The grief of God is not the grief of lost control, but the grief of violated relationship. This is covenantal sorrow. God grieves not because humanity has become inconvenient, but because it has become unwilling to be governed. Only a God who truly loves His creation can be wounded by what it has become.

Genesis is careful to show that God's assessment is moral, not emotional. The text does not rush from grief to destruction. It pauses. God sees. He evaluates. He names the condition of the world truthfully. The problem is not simply that humanity sins, but that sin has become continuous, defended, and internalized. Autonomy is no longer contested; it is assumed.

Judgment, then, is not God's abandonment of the world, but His refusal to allow evil to become eternal. A world that will not be governed cannot be sustained.

A civilization that celebrates violence cannot preserve life. To allow such a world to continue indefinitely would not be mercy; it would be abandonment.

Judgement as De-Creation

The form judgment takes in Genesis 6–7 is as instructive as the judgment itself. God does not introduce a novel instrument of destruction, nor does He act with improvisational force. Instead, He releases creation from the order that once held it together. Judgment comes not as annihilation, but as de-creation.

From the beginning, God ordered the world by separation and restraint. He divided the waters above from the waters below, set boundaries for the seas, and established limits that made life possible. Creation was not sustained by chaos held at bay through force, but by order upheld through God's continual governance. The world flourished because it remained responsive to His word.

Humanity rejected that order—not by dismantling creation directly, but by rejecting the authority that sustained it. Autonomy did not seek chaos; it sought independence. Yet independence from God does not produce freedom. It produces instability. When humanity refused God's ordering word, the world entrusted to human stewardship was inevitably affected.

The Flood is the physical manifestation of that moral rupture.

Genesis describes the collapse of the boundaries God once established. The "fountains of the great deep" are broken up, and the "windows of heaven" are opened. The waters above and below—once held apart by God's command—are released. Creation does not resist; it responds. The same world that once obeyed God's word now obeys His judgment.

This is not divine rage. It is tragic permission.

God allows the world to experience what autonomy ultimately demands: life without restraint. The Flood does not introduce chaos into a stable system; it reveals what the system becomes when God's sustaining order is withdrawn. The judgment corresponds precisely to the rebellion. Humanity dismantled moral boundaries; God releases physical ones. Violence filled the earth; waters now fill the earth.

The symmetry is deliberate.

Importantly, Genesis does not describe the Flood as an act of extermination. The earth is not destroyed by fire or erased into nothingness. It is submerged—returned temporarily to a state resembling Genesis 1:2, when the earth was "without form, and void," and darkness lay upon the face of the deep. Judgment returns creation to the edge of order, not beyond it.

This distinction matters deeply. God does not abandon His creation. He loosens it.

De-creation is not the undoing of God's purposes, but their preservation. A world organized around domination cannot sustain life indefinitely. A civilization that treats other image-bearers as expendable cannot remain habitable. To allow such a world to continue unchecked would not be mercy; it would be moral surrender. Judgment becomes the means by which God refuses to let evil become permanent.

Yet even in this loosening, restraint remains.

Genesis is careful to show that judgment is bounded. God does not erase humanity altogether. He does not eliminate animal life indiscriminately. He does not return the world to absolute nothingness. Preservation is woven into judgment from the beginning. Even as the waters rise, God is already acting with intention toward renewal.

This is why Scripture emphasizes that corruption had reached the point where "the earth was filled with violence." The problem is no longer individual wrongdoing, but systemic ruin. Creation itself has been drawn into humanity's rebellion—not because it has sinned, but because it has been subjected to a steward who refuses trust. The ground, once cursed because of Adam, now bears the weight of multiplied violence.

De-creation, then, is not arbitrary punishment. It is moral necessity. God intervenes not because the world has become inconvenient, but because it has become unlivable. Judgment halts a trajectory that would otherwise end in total collapse.

And still, God does not speak His final word here.

The Flood clears space—but it does not complete redemption. It restrains violence, but it does not heal the human heart. De-creation prepares the way for preservation, and preservation prepares the way for promise. Judgment is severe, but it is not ultimate. God will not allow autonomy to rule forever, but neither will He abandon the world to ruin.

The same God who releases the waters will soon speak again—not merely to judge, but to remember.

"But Noah Found Grace"

Against the darkness of Genesis 6 stands one of the most decisive and hope-laden sentences in all of Scripture:

> *"But Noah found grace in the eyes of the LORD."*

The contrast could not be sharper. Humanity has been described as continually oriented toward evil, its imagination corrupted and its will aligned with domination. Violence has become structural, and autonomy has succeeded in reshaping the world. And yet, grace interrupts the narrative. The sentence does not describe a reversal of human condition, but a divine initiative that breaks into inevitability.

It is essential to understand precisely what this statement means—and what it does not mean.

Scripture does not introduce Noah as a flawless man, a moral exception, or a heroic reformer standing above his generation. The text does not say Noah earned grace, deserved grace, or embodied grace. It says he found it. Grace, by definition, is not a reward discovered through effort, but a gift encountered through mercy. The initiative remains entirely God's.

This matters because Genesis is careful not to undermine its own diagnosis. Humanity has not improved. The human heart has not softened. Violence has not receded. Noah's presence does not signal that autonomy has failed; it signals that God has not abandoned His creation.

Grace precedes obedience.

Only after Noah is said to have found grace does Scripture describe him as "a just man and perfect in his generations," and as one who "walked with God."

These descriptions are not the cause of grace, but its fruit. To "walk with God" is not to achieve sinlessness, but to live in trust. It is directional language, not absolute language. Noah's life is oriented toward dependence in a world oriented toward autonomy.

This distinction guards us from a subtle but dangerous misunderstanding. Noah is not spared because he stands morally above his generation, as though God has found one worthy specimen to preserve. He is spared because God has chosen to preserve His purpose through grace rather than erase His creation through judgment alone.

Noah, then, is not a savior. He is a steward.

Scripture reinforces this by telling us that Noah was "perfect in his generations." The phrase does not imply moral flawlessness, but integrity within context. In a violent world ordered by domination, Noah lives differently. He does not seize power. He does not build a city. He does not secure his future through control. He walks with God. He trusts rather than grasps. His life bears witness not to human potential, but to divine mercy at work within human weakness.

This is why Genesis places Noah precisely where it does. Grace does not negate judgment; it accompanies it. Noah is not removed from the coming catastrophe. He will pass through it. The same waters that destroy the world will surround him. Grace does not spare Noah from the reality of judgment; it carries him through it.

Importantly, Noah is never presented as the solution to human sin. The narrative will soon make that painfully clear. After the Flood, Noah will fail. Sin will persist. The human heart will remain bent toward evil. Genesis refuses to romanticize Noah because it refuses to misplace hope. The preservation of the world does not depend on the moral strength of one man, but on the faithfulness of God.

What Noah represents, then, is not humanity redeemed, but humanity preserved. He stands as a transitional figure—a steward through whom God restrains violence and maintains continuity. The Flood will halt the trajectory of total collapse, but it will not heal the human heart. Grace will restrain, but it will not yet redeem.

This prepares the reader for what comes next. The salvation God provides through Noah is real, but it is provisional. It points forward rather than completing the story. A greater deliverance will be required—one that addresses not only violence in the world, but corruption in the heart.

For now, grace does what judgment alone cannot. It preserves the world so that God's purposes may continue. The story does not end with de-creation. It moves forward through grace—quietly, deliberately, and without spectacle.

God will not abandon His creation.

But neither will He ignore its ruin.

And so He calls Noah—not because Noah is the answer, but because grace has spoken.

The Ark: Obedient Refuge

Grace, when it appears in Scripture, does not remain abstract. It takes form. In the case of Noah, grace moves quickly from declaration to instruction. God does not merely announce preservation; He specifies how it will occur. Salvation is not left to human ingenuity, nor is it discovered through trial and error. It is given shape by God's word.

The ark is not Noah's idea. Scripture is careful on this point. God speaks, and Noah listens. Measurements are given. Materials are named. Proportions are specified. The precision of the instructions is striking, especially in a narrative that often moves with economy. Salvation is not improvised. It is ordered.

This matters because the ark stands in deliberate contrast to the structures humanity has already built east of Eden. Cain's city was an architectural response to fear—a human attempt to secure permanence without repentance. It was built to stabilize life on autonomous terms. The ark, by contrast, is built in submission. It is not a monument to human achievement, but a vessel of obedience.

Where the city sought control, the ark embodies trust.

Noah does not design the ark to withstand the Flood through superior engineering alone. He builds according to God's word, not because he understands every consequence, but because he trusts the One who speaks. Obedience precedes comprehension. Noah does not know precisely what the coming judgment will entail. He does not possess a map of the waters or a timeline of destruction. He has instruction—and that is enough.

The ark is therefore not a fortress against creation, but a refuge within it. It does not lift Noah above the world; it carries him through it. Salvation does not bypass the created order God declared good. It preserves it. The materials of the ark come from the same earth that will soon be submerged. Redemption works within creation, not against it.

This is underscored by what—and who—is brought into the ark. Noah is not preserved alone. Animals enter with him, "of every living thing of all flesh." Creation itself is carried through judgment. The steward who once fractured the relationship between humanity and the ground is now entrusted with preserving life through obedience. God's judgment is aimed at sin, not at the created order itself.

Scripture records only a single entrance into the ark. There are no barriers described, no guards appointed, no selective criteria imposed beyond God's word itself. The ark stands visible and accessible, constructed over time in the midst of a watching world. Judgment does not arrive without warning, nor does preservation occur in secret. The refuge God provides is neither hidden nor obscure. What separates those who are preserved from those who perish is not proximity, power, or privilege, but response to God's word. The text offers no suggestion that access was restricted by scarcity or withheld by design. The door stands open until the moment God Himself closes it.

The ark thus becomes a kind of mobile sanctuary—a space where God's ordering word still governs even as the world outside descends into chaos. Within the ark, boundaries remain. Distinctions are preserved. Life is ordered according to God's instruction. Outside the ark, the world experiences the consequences of rejecting that order.

Scripture repeatedly emphasizes Noah's response: "Thus did Noah; according to all that God commanded him, so did he." The repetition is intentional. Noah does not negotiate. He does not adjust the design to suit his preferences. He does not seek alternative solutions. In a world accustomed to redefining boundaries, Noah submits to them.

This obedience is not portrayed as heroic resolve or moral daring. It is quiet, persistent faithfulness. Noah builds over time, likely under scrutiny and misunderstanding, without public vindication or immediate reward. The text offers no speeches, no debates, no defenses. Obedience does not require explanation. It requires trust.

Importantly, the ark does not exist to prevent judgment. It exists to carry Noah through it. Grace does not cancel the Flood; it prepares a way through it. Noah will still hear the rain. He will still feel the rising waters. He will still experience the loss of the world he has known. Obedience does not exempt him from sorrow. It anchors him within it.

In this way, the ark becomes a visible testimony to the nature of grace. Grace does not promise escape from the consequences of sin; it promises preservation through them. It does not remove God's people from the groaning world; it carries them within it until renewal can begin.

Later Scripture describes Noah as "a preacher of righteousness," (2 Peter 2:5) which helps clarify what Genesis leaves understated. Noah's obedience was not mute. The construction of the ark itself stood as a sustained public testimony, but it was not the only one. Noah did not merely build; he bore witness. Righteousness was proclaimed, not invented. Judgment was announced, not improvised. Whatever form that proclamation took, it was sufficient to render the coming Flood neither sudden nor secret. The world was not destroyed without warning, and preservation was not offered without witness. What went unheeded was not a lack of information, but a refusal of trust.

The ark stands as a rebuke to autonomy and a witness to trust. Where autonomy seeks safety through control, grace provides refuge through obedience. Where self-rule builds monuments to permanence, faith builds vessels of preservation. The difference is not architectural; it is theological.

God does not save the world through human mastery, but through human submission to His word.

The ark floats not because it is clever, but because it is obedient.

Passing Through Judgment

When the Flood finally comes, Scripture is careful to remove any sense of surprise. The rain does not fall suddenly upon an unsuspecting world. The ark stands completed. Noah and his household enter. The animals gather. Time passes. The coming judgment has been announced, witnessed, and patiently delayed. When it arrives, it does so deliberately.

The text marks the moment with sober restraint:

"And the LORD shut him in."

This single statement carries enormous theological weight. Until this point, the ark has stood accessible. The refuge God provided was visible, proclaimed, and unhidden. Now the door is closed—not by Noah, but by God Himself. Judgment does not begin when the rain falls; it begins when God seals the means of preservation. The time for response has ended.

This moment is neither arbitrary nor cruel. It is necessary. A door that never closes ceases to be a door at all. Restraint delayed indefinitely becomes abandonment. God's act of closing the ark is not the withdrawal of mercy, but the confirmation that mercy has been refused. The period of warning has run its course.

What follows is devastating in scope and quiet in description. The fountains of the deep break forth. The windows of heaven open. Waters rise steadily, relentlessly, without commentary or pause. Genesis does not dramatize the suffering, but neither does it minimize it. The destruction is total in its reach. Life outside the ark perishes.

Noah is not spared the experience of judgment. He hears the rain. He feels the ark lift from the ground. He is carried into the same waters that destroy the world he has known. The righteous are not preserved *from* judgment, but *through* it. Grace does not remove Noah from the groaning of creation; it sustains him within it.

This distinction is crucial. Obedience does not insulate Noah from sorrow. He does not float above the Flood untouched by its cost. Preservation is not painless. The ark becomes a place of confinement as much as refuge—a vessel sealed against chaos, but also cut off from the world outside. Salvation involves loss as well as life.

Genesis emphasizes the duration of the Flood to make this point clear. Judgment is not momentary. The waters prevail. Days stretch into months. Waiting becomes part of obedience. Noah cannot shorten the ordeal or control its outcome. He is carried entirely by what God has provided.

Yet within the ark, order remains.

Boundaries still exist. Life is sustained. The same God who loosened the world's foundations continues to uphold the space He has set apart. Judgment and preservation operate simultaneously. The waters that destroy also lift. The ark floats not because the Flood is gentle, but because God remains faithful.

This paradox lies at the heart of biblical judgment. God does not suspend the consequences of sin for His people; He bears them through it. The Flood is not selective punishment that avoids the righteous; it is a reality that all must face, either exposed or sheltered by grace.

Genesis does not invite the reader to imagine rescue scenarios or last-minute reversals. The focus remains fixed on God's action and Noah's trust. Once the door is closed, the narrative moves forward inexorably. Judgment proceeds, and preservation holds.

The world outside the ark is undone. The world within it is sustained—not because it is stronger, wiser, or more deserving, but because it rests entirely upon what God has spoken and built.

Passing through judgment is not triumphal. It is humbling. Noah survives not as a conqueror, but as a witness to the truth that life cannot be preserved apart from trust. The Flood exposes the lie of autonomy and confirms the necessity of dependence.

What God destroys is violence.

What He preserves is life.

And He does both without haste, without excess, and without regret.

Remembered by God

After the waters have prevailed, after months of confinement and waiting, Scripture introduces one of its most understated and powerful transitions:

"And God remembered Noah."

This is not the language of forgetfulness corrected. It is covenant language. To be remembered by God is not to reenter His awareness, but to become the object of His faithful action. God's remembrance signals not a change of mind, but the unfolding of intention. Judgment has run its course; preservation now moves toward renewal.

The movement from de-creation to re-creation begins quietly. There is no command, no thunderous declaration, no dramatic reversal. Instead, "God made a wind to pass over the earth, and the waters assuaged." The imagery deliberately echoes the opening of Genesis, where the Spirit of God moved upon the face of the waters. The world is not created again by force, but restored through God's sustaining presence.

The waters recede slowly. Scripture marks time carefully—days, months, seasons passing. Renewal does not rush. The patience that marked God's restraint before judgment now marks His restraint after it. The world is given space to reemerge, just as it was once given space to repent.

Noah's response mirrors this patience. He does not seize control of the moment or force his way into the new world. He waits. He sends forth birds, watching, discerning, learning when the earth is ready to bear life again. Trust expresses itself not in action alone, but in restraint. Noah does not rush where God has not yet spoken.

When the ground is finally dry, Noah still waits for God's word. Only after God commands does he leave the ark. Renewal does not belong to human initiative. The same obedience that built the ark now governs its departure. Preservation continues until God Himself declares the time complete.

The first act Noah performs in the renewed world is worship. Before planting, before building, before securing the future, Noah offers sacrifice. Worship precedes settlement. Dependence precedes dominion. The restored world begins not with productivity, but with acknowledgment.

This act of worship is not an attempt to manipulate God or secure favor. It is recognition. Noah responds to preservation with gratitude rather than entitlement. He does not assume the world is his by right. He receives it again as a gift.

God's response reveals the deeper purpose of remembrance. The Lord declares that He will not again curse the ground in the same way, even though "the imagination of man's heart is evil from his youth." This admission is critical. Renewal has not healed the human heart. The Flood restrained violence, but it did not redeem desire. And yet, God binds Himself to the world anyway.

This is the turning point of the narrative. God does not preserve the world because humanity has improved. He preserves it because He chooses to sustain it. The future of creation will not rest on human reliability, but on divine promise.

The rhythm of the world is reestablished—seedtime and harvest, cold and heat, summer and winter. Order returns, not because chaos has been defeated forever, but because God has committed Himself to maintaining it. The groaning world will continue, but it will not be abandoned.

Genesis 8 teaches us that renewal does not erase the past, nor does it deny reality. It proceeds with full knowledge of human frailty. God remembers Noah, not because Noah is the solution, but because grace remains God's chosen means of preservation.

The waters have receded.

The ground is restored.

The heart remains unchanged.

And still, God continues.

The Acceleration of Natural Evil

The Flood does more than judge moral corruption. It permanently alters the conditions under which life must now be lived.

Before the Flood, Scripture presents a world marked by human violence but relative environmental stability. Evil is moral and relational. Humanity sins against humanity. Blood cries from the ground, but the ground itself does not yet turn violently against its inhabitants. The earth resists labor, but it remains broadly hospitable to life. Judgment, when it comes, moves primarily through human hands.

After the Flood, this changes.

Genesis does not describe the post-Flood world as cursed anew, but it unmistakably portrays it as harsher, less predictable, and more dangerous. God now speaks of seasons as fixed cycles rather than effortless continuities. Cold and heat, seedtime and harvest, summer and winter are named explicitly—as though stability itself now requires divine governance. The implication is subtle but profound: the world no longer simply gives life; it must be managed.

The waters that once sustained creation have now become agents of destruction. The dew which once watered the ground becomes rain which washes away the topsoil. Humanity steps into a world where the same forces that sustain life can now erase it without warning. Floods, storms, droughts, and environmental upheaval become part of the human horizon—not as targeted moral judgments, but as features of a creation that has been violently reordered.

This does not mean creation has become malicious or autonomous. Scripture never presents nature as an independent enemy, nor as a rival power to God. Rather, it presents a world in which harmony diminishes as rebellion multiplies. As humanity presses creation into service apart from God, the alignment between Creator, creature, and creation fractures. The Flood functions as a necessary cleansing, but cleansing under judgment does not restore ease—it introduces greater testing. Creation remains governed by God, yet its systems now operate under strain. The earth still functions, but it does so imperfectly, sometimes violently.

From this point forward, humanity contends not only with sin and violence, but with a world that can harm indiscriminately. Earthquakes do not ask permission. Drought does not distinguish between the righteous and the wicked. Disease spreads without moral discernment. Famine follows failed harvests. Storms collapse homes without regard for virtue. Suffering is no longer confined to the realm of choice; it is woven into experience.

The distinction between moral and natural evil becomes clearer here. Moral evil arises from human will—from rebellion, domination, and violence deliberately chosen. Natural evil arises from a world whose harmony has been disrupted by judgment. The two are not identical, but they are inseparable. Humanity sins; creation suffers—and in its suffering, humanity now suffers alongside it.

Evil has multiplied. What began as rebellion in the garden has spread into violence between brothers, domination through culture, and now danger embedded in the environment itself. Evil no longer requires human permission to harm.

Yet even here, mercy remains. The same covenant that restrains future cosmic judgment also ensures the continuation of seasons, harvests, and life. The world is harsher, but it is still held. Broken, but governed. Dangerous, but not abandoned.

The Flood does not explain every disaster. It explains why a good creation is no longer safe.

Covenant with a Groaning Creation

With the waters receded and the earth restored, Genesis does not turn to human resolve or renewed moral confidence. The future of the world is not entrusted to improved behavior, collective memory, or the hope that humanity has finally learned its lesson.

Instead, God speaks again—and what He speaks is covenant.

The language is deliberate and emphatic. God establishes His covenant not as a negotiated agreement, but as a unilateral commitment. Noah offers no pledge of obedience. Humanity gives no assurance of reform. God binds Himself fully aware of what the human heart remains. The imagination that produced violence before the Flood has not been healed by it. The world has been preserved, not purified.

This is precisely what makes the covenant so striking.

God explicitly acknowledges that "the imagination of man's heart is evil from his youth," and yet He commits Himself to the continued stability of the world anyway. Preservation is not granted because humanity has improved, but because God chooses restraint over annihilation. Judgment has done its necessary work; now promise sets the terms of the future.

Even more significant is the scope of that promise. God does not bind Himself only to Noah, nor even only to humanity. The covenant is established "with every living creature of all flesh." Birds, livestock, beasts of the earth—all are named as recipients of divine commitment. Creation itself is drawn into the covenantal relationship.

This matters because creation has suffered without choosing rebellion. The ground bore the weight of human violence. The waters swept away innocent life along with the guilty. Now God addresses creation not as a culprit, but as something He refuses to abandon. The groaning world is not dismissed; it is assured.

The covenant does not promise the absence of suffering, but it does promise continuity. Seedtime and harvest will remain. Seasons will endure. Life will proceed within an ordered framework sustained by God's faithfulness. Chaos will no longer be permitted to consume the earth unchecked.

The sign of this covenant makes the point unmistakable. God places His bow in the clouds. In the ancient world, the bow is a weapon—an instrument of judgment. Here, it is set aside, turned away from the earth. Judgment is not abolished, but it is restrained. The weapon remains, but it is no longer aimed.

This image reveals something essential about God's posture toward the world. The covenant is not merely a promise to humanity; it is a self-limitation undertaken by God Himself. He binds His own action to patience. He commits to preservation even in the face of continued human failure.

Notably, the sign is given as much for God's remembrance as for humanity's reassurance. The bow in the clouds stands as a declaration of divine resolve. God will remember His covenant even when humanity forgets its calling. The endurance of the world rests not on human consistency, but on divine faithfulness.

At the same time, the covenant does not dissolve moral responsibility. Human life is explicitly protected. Violence is named and restrained. Stewardship is reaffirmed rather than revoked. God preserves the world without surrendering His authority over it. Restraint does not mean permission.

Genesis 9 thus becomes the theological center of the Flood narrative. Judgment has halted a trajectory of total collapse. Grace has preserved life through the waters. Now covenant stabilizes the future. The world will continue—not because it is healed, but because it is held.

Creation will still groan. Humanity will still struggle. Sin will still distort desire. Yet history will move forward under promise rather than threat. The answer to the world's continued existence is not progress, but patience—not human virtue, but divine commitment.

God binds Himself to a groaning creation, not because it is worthy, but because He intends to redeem it.

Still Broken, Yet Held

The narrative of the Flood does not end in triumph. Genesis refuses to allow the reader to mistake preservation for transformation or restraint for redemption. Almost immediately after the covenant is established, Scripture returns our attention to the human heart—and what it reveals is continuity rather than cure.

Noah emerges from the ark not as a new Adam, but as the same man who entered it. He plants a vineyard. He drinks. He becomes drunk. He lies uncovered in his tent. The details are spare, but the implication is unmistakable. The Flood has not healed the human condition. The world has been stabilized, but the heart remains vulnerable, disordered, and capable of shame.

The text offers no excuses and no embellishment. Noah's failure is recorded without comment or mitigation. This is not the fall of a hero, but the exposure of a truth Genesis has been careful to maintain: judgment can restrain violence, but it cannot reform desire. The imagination remains bent. The will remains fragile. The problem diagnosed before the Flood persists after it.

The behavior of Noah's sons reinforces this reality. One responds to his father's exposure with disregard and display; the others respond with restraint and care. Even within a single family preserved through judgment, moral divergence appears immediately. Violence has been curtailed, but virtue has not been secured. Preservation has created space for life to continue, not a guarantee of righteousness.

This moment is crucial for understanding the covenant that precedes it. God did not bind Himself to a healed humanity, but to a broken one. He preserved the world with full knowledge of what it would remain. The covenant was never a declaration that sin had been resolved, but a commitment that history would not be abandoned.

Genesis places this failure where it does for a reason. It prevents the Flood from being misread as a solution rather than a restraint. The waters halted a trajectory of total collapse, but they did not produce a new humanity. The same capacities that led to violence before the Flood remain active afterward. The difference now is not the heart of man, but the promise of God.

This is what it means for the world to be held.

The earth continues not because it is righteous, but because it is under covenant. Life persists not because humanity has learned to govern itself rightly, but because God has chosen patience over annihilation. The world is stable, not because chaos has been defeated, but because God restrains it.

This restraint, however, does not eliminate consequence. The brokenness of the human heart continues to shape families, cultures, and history. Shame, conflict, and division reappear almost immediately. Genesis does not sanitize this reality. It names it quietly and moves forward.

Still, the narrative does not descend into despair. The point is not that humanity is beyond hope, but that hope will not come through judgment alone. Preservation makes space for redemption; it does not accomplish it. The covenant holds the world steady while something greater is prepared.

The Flood teaches that God will not allow evil to rule unchecked, but it also teaches that evil cannot be cured by force. The problem is deeper than behavior and more stubborn than environment. What is required is not another reset, but a new heart.

And yet, God remains faithful.

The world after the Flood is neither restored Eden nor abandoned ruin. It is a groaning creation—fractured, exposed, and still capable of harm—yet held within the patience of God. History will continue under restraint rather than resolution, promise rather than perfection.

The story moves forward not because humanity has been fixed, but because God has chosen to remain.

Summary

Genesis 6–9 presents the Flood not as an emotional outburst or a failed experiment, but as a necessary act of restraint within a world spiraling toward total collapse. Human autonomy had matured into violence, domination, and cultural normalization of evil. Judgment did not interrupt a healthy world; it halted a trajectory that could no longer sustain life.

Yet the Flood also reveals what judgment cannot do. It can restrain violence, but it cannot reform the human heart. It can reset conditions, but it cannot restore harmony. The imagination of humanity remains bent toward self-rule even after the waters recede. Preservation does not equal healing.

The world that emerges after the Flood is altered. Creation continues under divine governance, but now under strain. Moral evil persists, and natural danger accelerates. Humanity contends not only with sin and violence, but with a creation that no longer reliably shelters life. Suffering becomes woven into experience rather than limited to choice.

Into this fractured reality, God establishes a covenant. He binds Himself to a groaning creation—not because it is redeemed, but because He refuses to abandon it. Judgment gives way to patience. Chaos is restrained. History is permitted to continue.

The Flood, then, is not the solution to the problem of evil. It is the acknowledgment that evil must be restrained until it can be redeemed. The world is preserved, not perfected. Managed, not healed.

Genesis 6–9 does not end the groaning of creation. It ensures that the groaning will not end creation itself. The story moves forward under promise rather than threat, awaiting a redemption judgment alone could never achieve.

4

When We Break It Further

Sin After Restraint

The Flood restrained violence, but it did not restrain the human will. Almost immediately, Genesis demonstrates that judgment does not cure rebellion; it merely interrupts its momentum. Noah's failure after the Flood is not presented as a shocking deviation, but as confirmation of continuity. The same heart that required restraint before the waters remains after them. Sin does not reemerge slowly or cautiously—it resumes as soon as opportunity allows. The preserved world is still governed by fragile and disordered desires.

From Wandering to Walls

The first city in Scripture does not arise from blessing, abundance, or creative flourishing. It arises from judgment. Cain builds a city only after he has been confronted for murder, only after he has rejected God's warning, and only after he has been told that his future will be marked by wandering. The city is not Cain's contribution to civilization; it is his response to fear.

God tells Cain that he will be "a fugitive and a vagabond on the earth." Cain hears not a call to dependence, but a threat to security. His immediate concern is not repentance, but vulnerability. He fears exposure. He fears instability. He fears a life that must be lived without walls. And so, rather than trusting the God who marks him for protection, Cain seeks permanence on his own terms. He builds a city.

The act is profoundly theological. Cain does not simply construct shelter; he constructs an alternative vision of safety. The city becomes a refusal of wandering, a denial of creaturely dependence, and a declaration that permanence can be achieved without trust. Architecture replaces obedience. Stone replaces faith. What Cain builds is not merely a place to live, but a strategy to manage life apart from God.

Scripture is remarkably restrained in its description, but the placement is unmistakable. The city is Cain's answer to judgment. Where God declared movement, Cain establishes consolidation. Where God imposed vulnerability, Cain manufactures control. The city is not neutral ground; it is an act of resistance.

This pattern will repeat.

From the beginning, rebellion does not always express itself as chaos. More often, it expresses itself as order of the wrong kind. Cain does not descend into lawlessness; he organizes. He names the city after his son, anchoring identity in lineage rather than calling. The future is secured not by promise, but by continuity of blood and brick. The city becomes a way of saying, I will endure, even if I must do so without God.

In this way, the city functions as a counterfeit of divine provision. God had promised Cain protection, but Cain seeks protection he can see. God had declared boundaries for his life, but Cain redraws them in stone. The city becomes a visible assurance meant to quiet an anxious heart that will not rest in divine word alone.

This does not mean that cities are inherently evil, nor that human creativity is itself rebellion. Scripture will later acknowledge cities, regulate them, and even use them. But Cain's city sets the tone. Urban consolidation enters the biblical story not as fulfillment of God's design, but as an adaptation to judgment. It is born not of gratitude, but of fear.

What is most telling is what the city attempts to prevent. Cain builds in order not to wander. He gathers life inward rather than receiving it outward.

The city becomes a means of resisting dispersion, of stabilizing existence apart from trust. This instinct—to gather, to fortify, to centralize—is not accidental. It reflects a heart that no longer believes that life can be sustained through obedience alone.

Later cities will grow more complex, more powerful, and more sophisticated, but they will inherit this same impulse. From Cain forward, the city will repeatedly serve as humanity's attempt to secure permanence without submission, unity without dependence, and identity without reference to God.

The first city, then, is not a milestone of progress, but a marker of direction. It reveals how rebellion reorganizes human life. What begins as a refusal to trust becomes a built environment. Fear becomes architecture. Autonomy becomes spatial.

And once rebellion takes form in stone, it is far harder to undo.God's Pattern of Distribution

Against humanity's repeated instinct toward concentration, Scripture consistently presents a different vision of life. God's ideal is not dense consolidation, but distributed stewardship—"every man under his own vine and fig tree." Stability is grounded in land, family, and local provision rather than centralized power. Even when cities are permitted, they are restrained. The Levitical cities are deliberately limited, dispersed, and surrounded by open land. Sacred service is prevented from becoming urban dominance. God tolerates cities, but He never idealizes them.

Vines, Fig Trees, and the Shape of Trust

Against humanity's repeated instinct toward consolidation, Scripture presents a markedly different vision of life—one grounded in distribution, limitation, and trust. God's response to rebellion is not an immediate abolition of cities, but the persistent articulation of an alternative way of inhabiting the world. That vision is captured most simply, and most enduringly, in the image that appears again and again throughout the Old Testament: every man under his own vine and under his own fig tree.

The image is deliberately modest. It does not describe wealth, dominance, or expansion. It describes sufficiency. A vine and a fig tree require time to mature. They root a family to a place without enclosing it behind walls. They provide provision without accumulation, stability without centralization. Life under vine and fig tree is local, embodied, and dependent upon rhythms God sustains rather than systems humanity controls.

This vision stands in quiet contrast to the logic of the city as Cain first conceived it. Where the city gathers life inward, God disperses it outward. Where the city secures permanence through density, God establishes stability through inheritance. Land is not seized; it is received. Identity is not manufactured through proximity and power, but cultivated through faithfulness over time. The good life is not built quickly, nor fortified against risk, but grown patiently within limits.

Even when Scripture permits cities, it does so with careful restraint. The most revealing example is the arrangement of the Levitical cities. The Levites are given cities not as centers of political or economic dominance, but as places of service scattered among the tribes. Their cities are limited in size, surrounded by open land, and deliberately prevented from becoming engines of accumulation. Sacred authority is distributed rather than centralized. Even worship is guarded against becoming a means of control.

This restraint reveals something essential about God's concern. The problem is not community, cooperation, or shared life. The problem is consolidation that removes life from the limits God designed. When people cluster too tightly, power concentrates. When power concentrates, accountability diminishes. When accountability diminishes, both moral and natural consequences multiply. What begins as efficiency quietly becomes domination.

The prophets later give voice to this same concern. Isaiah pronounces judgment not against labor or land itself, but against accumulation without limit: "Woe unto them that join house to house, that lay field to field, till there be no place." (Isaiah 5:8). The problem is not productivity, but compression. Life is gathered inward until there is no room left—for rest, for dependence, or for restraint. What God intended to be stewarded becomes something to be consumed and controlled.

God's pattern of distribution functions, then, as a form of protection. It slows the spread of violence. It limits the reach of failure. It ensures that no single human system becomes indispensable to survival. Life remains fragile enough to require trust, but stable enough to endure. Dependence is not eliminated; it is properly directed.

This distributed vision also honors the created order itself. Land is allowed to rest. Families are embedded in place. Human life remains close to soil, seasons, and the limits of creatureliness. The world is not bent to human will through scale and concentration, but stewarded through presence and restraint. Creation groans less where it is not overburdened.

What is striking is how often humanity resists this vision. Dispersion feels unsafe. Difference feels threatening. Dependence feels risky. Consolidation promises security, identity, and permanence without the vulnerability of trust. And so the impulse toward gathering, fortifying, and centralizing reasserts itself— not because it is wiser, but because it feels safer.

In this light, the city becomes not merely a location, but a philosophy. It promises safety through proximity, identity through uniformity, and endurance through scale. God's alternative promises life through patience, obedience, and trust within limits. The tension between these two visions—distributed stewardship and consolidated control—will shape everything that follows.

By the time humanity arrives at Babel, this tension will no longer be subtle. The city will no longer be a response to individual fear, but a shared ideology. What Cain attempted alone, Babel will attempt together. And what God restrained through instruction, He will soon restrain through intervention.

As human life becomes increasingly concentrated, the consequences of rebellion do not merely persist; they multiply. Cities do not create evil, but they accelerate its effects. When God's design for distributed stewardship is abandoned in favor of density and consolidation, both moral and natural consequences intensify—not because creation becomes vindictive, but because it is burdened beyond the limits for which it was ordered.

The Weight of Density

From the beginning, human rebellion has altered not only behavior, but environment. When people gather in unnatural proximity, the conditions of life change. Animals are brought closer to human dwellings. Waste accumulates faster than it can be absorbed. Water sources are shared, contaminated, and stressed. Illness that once remained local now spreads quickly and indiscriminately. The world itself begins to groan under the weight of human reorganization.

This does not require the language of punishment to be understood. Disease is not a moral agent, nor is biology a courtroom. What Scripture presents is consequence, not condemnation. When humanity insists on reshaping life according to fear and control rather than trust and restraint, the created order responds according to its nature. What once functioned within balance becomes unstable when pressed into density.

Urban concentration places human and animal life into sustained proximity that did not exist in God's original pattern. For most of human history prior to large-scale settlement, people lived dispersed across land, with limited and irregular contact with animals beyond hunting or small-scale husbandry. Under those conditions, truly life-threatening infectious disease appears to have been rare. Illness existed, injury existed, and death existed, but the kind of widespread, rapidly fatal disease that later defined human experience required a different environment to emerge.

That environment developed as humans began to cluster densely and to live in constant proximity to domesticated animals and urban pests. Through what is now called *zoonotic transmission*, diseases adapted to animal hosts, such as tuberculosis (cattle), influenza (birds or pigs), plague (rats), and typhus (lice), crossed species boundaries and entered the human population. What an animal could tolerate easily—often without serious harm—proved devastating to human bodies with no prior exposure or resistance. Rats, livestock, and insects became carriers not by malice, but by proximity. Infection began to travel faster than care could respond.

This helps explain not only the vulnerability of later urban populations, but also the extraordinary longevity described in the earliest chapters of Genesis. A world with limited density, minimal cross-species exposure, and greater environmental stability would not have subjected the human body to the same relentless biological pressures that emerged later. As human settlement patterns changed, the conditions of life changed with them. Disease did not suddenly appear as judgment; it accelerated as consequence.

Vulnerability increased not because the earth had become hostile, but because it had been asked to bear more than it was designed to carry. Creation does not rebel; it strains.

Sanitation, too, becomes a silent witness to this strain. Waste that could once be absorbed by land and time is compressed into narrow spaces. The rhythms of cleansing built into soil, water, and rest are disrupted. The result is not immediate collapse, but cumulative fragility. Small failures ripple outward. Contagion becomes systemic. What was once survivable becomes catastrophic under scale.

In this way, natural evil is not introduced by human sin, but accelerated by it. The Flood restrained moral violence, but it did not reverse humanity's impulse to consolidate. As cities grow, the world grows harsher — not because God has withdrawn His care, but because the conditions under which care operates have been altered. Life becomes more precarious, more exposed, more vulnerable to forces beyond human control.

This acceleration reshapes human experience profoundly. Suffering becomes less predictable and less personal. It is no longer tied directly to individual action or choice. The righteous and the wicked alike are affected. Disease does not distinguish motive. Famine does not assess intent. Creation groans not in judgment, but in fatigue.

What emerges is a world increasingly marked by shared fragility. Humanity is confronted with limits it cannot engineer away. Systems designed to secure life instead magnify risk. Control promises safety but delivers complexity. The very structures meant to stabilize existence introduce new forms of vulnerability.

This is not to suggest that God's concern lies in reversing human progress or dismantling society. The issue is not complexity itself, but consolidation without restraint. When life is compressed beyond its created capacity, consequence accelerates. The earth bears witness not through moral outrage, but through breakdown.

By the time humanity arrives at Babel, this acceleration is already underway. The city has become more than a shelter; it is now a worldview. The desire to centralize, to unify, to secure permanence through proximity has taken hold. What Cain built to quiet fear, Babel will build to establish identity. And what has already begun to strain creation will soon threaten the future of humanity itself.

The Architecture of Defiance

By the time humanity arrives at Babel, the city is no longer merely a response to individual fear or environmental pressure. It has become an idea—a shared conviction about how life should be secured. What Cain built to quiet his own vulnerability, Babel builds to establish collective identity. The city is no longer accidental. It is intentional, ideological, and ambitious.

Genesis describes a world unified by language and purpose. This unity is often mistaken for virtue, but the text does not present it as such. The problem is not communication, but unanimity. Humanity speaks with one voice because it has chosen one vision of life— one that resists dispersion, dependence, and distinction. The command to fill the earth is quietly set aside in favor of remaining together. Uniformity replaces obedience.

The materials and methods matter. Humanity builds with brick rather than stone, tar rather than mortar. What God once provided through creation is now manufactured through technique. The city rises not from the land as gift, but from human ingenuity as assertion. This is not simply construction; it is self-authorship. Life is no longer received. It is engineered.

At the heart of Babel's project is a desire for permanence without trust. "Let us make a name for ourselves," they say, "lest we be scattered." The fear is explicit. Dispersion is experienced not as calling, but as a threat. To be spread across the earth would require dependence—on God, on land not yet known, on futures not yet secured. Babel offers an alternative: stability through proximity, meaning through scale, endurance through collective strength, identity in achievement.

The tower itself is not an attempt to storm heaven, but to manage destiny. It represents humanity's desire to control time, fate, and identity from a fixed center. Heaven is observed, measured, and consulted rather than trusted. The tower stands as a symbol of life oriented upward without submission—transcendence without worship.

Genesis responds with deliberate irony. "The Lord came down to see the city and the tower." What humanity exalts does not impress. What is presented as greatness requires divine condescension even to be observed. The issue is not threat, but trajectory. God does not say that the project is too powerful, but that it is too unified in the wrong direction. If humanity remains consolidated in rebellion, its capacity for harm will outpace its capacity for restraint.

God's intervention is subtle and severe at the same time. He does not destroy the city. He does not strike the builders. He confuses their language. Communication fractures, cooperation dissolves, and the project collapses under its own weight. The judgment is not annihilation, but limitation. What obedience would have produced slowly—diversity, dispersion, differentiation—God now brings about swiftly.

This scattering is not a curse. **It is mercy**. A humanity unified in autonomy would become ungovernable and increasingly destructive. Fragmentation preserves the future. By breaking the project, God protects both creation and humanity from the consequences of unchecked consolidation. Diversity is not introduced as punishment, but restored as design.

Babel names the city that humanity abandons, but the impulse does not disappear. The desire to gather, to fortify, to unify life under human control will resurface again and again throughout history. Babel is not a single failure; it is a pattern revealed.

What Genesis makes clear is that God will not allow the world to be secured through fear-driven unity. Identity will not be stabilized through scale. Permanence will not be achieved through consolidation. When humanity insists on building life around control rather than trust, God intervenes—not to destroy the world, but to keep it from destroying itself.

Babel marks the moment when the city becomes a shared rebellion rather than an individual refuge. It is the culmination of a trajectory that began with Cain and intensified through density and strain. From this point forward, the tension between human cities and God's purposes will define the shape of history—until a different city, built by God rather than seized by humanity, finally brings that tension to rest.

Summary

Genesis 9–11 reveals that restraint does not end rebellion; it reshapes it. Sin reemerges almost immediately after the Flood, not as unrestrained violence, but as reorganization. What judgment curtails in chaos, humanity recovers through structure, consolidation, and control.

The city becomes the primary expression of this shift. Cain's city answers fear with permanence. Distributed life under vine and fig tree is set aside in favor of density and proximity. What begins as a search for safety quietly becomes a philosophy of life—one that gathers people inward, compresses space, and seeks endurance through scale rather than trust.

As life is concentrated, consequence accelerates. Creation itself is strained under new conditions. Disease spreads where proximity erodes natural boundaries. Vulnerability increases not because the earth turns hostile, but because it is burdened beyond its design. Natural evil is not introduced, but intensified. The world begins to groan under human reorganization.

Babel marks the culmination of this trajectory. The city is no longer a refuge but an ideology. Humanity unites not to obey but to secure identity and permanence apart from God. Unity without submission becomes dangerous. God intervenes not to destroy but to restrain—fracturing language, dispersing peoples, and preserving the future through limitation.

Genesis does not present these developments as isolated failures but as a pattern. Rebellion matures from individual autonomy into shared structure. What cannot be sustained through violence alone is stabilized through consolidation. The city becomes the means by which fear is managed and control is maintained.

The story does not end with Babel but it changes direction. Humanity will continue to build, gather, and organize. The question is no longer whether rebellion will persist but how it will express itself when given permanence and power.

The World Made New

5

From City to Empire: Nimrod and the Rise of Power

Genesis 10 is often treated as background material—a table of names inserted between more dramatic stories. But its placement is deliberate. Where Genesis 11 reveals the restraint of human unity at Babel, Genesis 10 reveals what emerges alongside and after that restraint: the rise of power. The city stabilizes rebellion; empire enforces it. In Nimrod, Scripture introduces not merely a builder but a ruler—the first figure to turn consolidation into domination.

Nimrod: The Personalization of Power

Cain built a city, but Nimrod builds authority. Genesis does not describe Nimrod primarily by what he constructs but by who he becomes: "a mighty one in the earth." Power is no longer shared or incidental; it is embodied. Rebellion moves from collective impulse into personal rule. What Babel attempted through unanimity, Nimrod advances through hierarchy.

"A Mighty Hunter Before the LORD"

The city stabilizes rebellion, but it does not yet rule. As long as power remains diffuse, resistance is possible, and accountability remains local. Genesis marks a decisive change when rebellion takes on a human face—when consolidation is no longer merely shared but embodied. In Nimrod, power becomes personal.

Scripture introduces Nimrod not through genealogy or lineage but through distinction: "He began to be a mighty one in the earth." This is not the language of craft or cultivation but of dominance. Nimrod does not simply participate in the world as it is; he reshapes it through strength. Authority is no longer incidental to social life. It becomes central.

This is a critical development. Where Babel attempted unity through unanimity, Nimrod advances control through hierarchy. Power is no longer something exercised collectively or situationally; it is gathered, concentrated, and wielded by a figure who stands above others. Rebellion matures from shared refusal into enforced order.

The text does not say that Nimrod was appointed. He is not described as chosen, called, or entrusted. He becomes mighty. Power is seized rather than given. This distinction matters. Biblical authority is always derivative and accountable. Nimrod's authority is self-originating. It exists because he has the strength to impose it.

In this way, Nimrod represents a fundamental shift in human organization. The city provided permanence. Power now provides direction. What had been a shared project now becomes a governed one. The logic of empire requires not merely proximity but leadership that can compel obedience and suppress fracture. Authority is no longer relational; it is structural.

This personalization of power changes how rebellion expresses itself. No longer does humanity simply gather in fear; it submits in exchange for stability. Order is achieved, but at a cost. Dependence shifts away from God and toward the ruler. Trust is relocated from promise to protection. The ruler becomes the guarantor of life's coherence.

Genesis offers no moral commentary at this point, only description. But the silence is instructive. Scripture allows the pattern to speak for itself. When power becomes centralized in a person, rebellion gains durability. What once required collective agreement can now be enforced through command. The city no longer needs unanimity. It needs loyalty.

This development also explains why empire emerges so quickly once power is personalized. A centralized figure cannot remain local for long. Authority seeks territory. Control presses outward. What begins as leadership inevitably becomes domination when untethered from submission to God. The ruler must expand, or risk being replaced.

Nimrod, then, is not introduced as a villain in the dramatic sense, but as a turning point. He is the first figure in Scripture to embody authority detached from stewardship. Through him, rebellion gains direction, momentum, and permanence. The city has found its ruler.

From this point forward, the story of humanity will repeatedly return to this pattern. Wherever consolidation hardens into control, a Nimrod figure emerges. The names will change. The cultures will differ. But the structure remains the same. Power, once personalized, reshapes the world.

From City to Kingdom

A city can exist without ruling beyond itself, but a kingdom cannot. The moment power is centralized in a person, the city is no longer merely inhabited—it is governed. Genesis marks this transition with deliberate clarity: "The beginning of his kingdom was Babel." What had been a place now becomes a seat. What had been shared now becomes commanded.

Babel was built through collective will. Again and again the text emphasizes the language of unanimity: "let us build," "let us make a name." Authority at Babel was diffuse, persuasion mattered, and unity depended on agreement. The project could continue only so long as the people chose together to resist dispersion. When language fractured, consensus collapsed, and the city fell silent.

Empire marks a decisive shift. What Babel required through consent, Nimrod secures through rule. Authority no longer rests in collective decision, but in a person who commands. Rebellion no longer depends on unanimity; it endures through hierarchy. The city no longer needs agreement to persist. It needs loyalty.

This shift is subtle but decisive. A city gathers people; a kingdom organizes them. Authority no longer emerges from proximity or custom, but flows outward from a center. Law replaces shared practice.

Command replaces cooperation. The city becomes the nucleus of something larger, something that cannot remain contained.

Empire arises not because rulers are uniquely ambitious, but because consolidation creates pressure. Density demands management. Management requires enforcement. Enforcement, in turn, requires reach. Once authority is centralized, it must either expand or fracture. The logic of empire is not excess—it is inevitability.

Genesis traces this movement with restraint. Nimrod's kingdom begins at Babel, but it does not end there. From that center, authority extends into Assyria, giving rise to Nineveh and other cities. Expansion is not presented as conquest alone, but as continuation. Power radiates outward, incorporating new territories and peoples under a single rule. What began as consolidation becomes domination.

This development changes the nature of human life profoundly. Under kingdom rule, individuals are no longer primarily stewards of land and family, but subjects of authority. Identity shifts from inheritance to allegiance. Security is no longer grounded in God's provision, but in the strength of the ruler. The king becomes the guarantor of order.

Empire also reshapes space. Land is no longer received as a gift, but measured, claimed, and administered. Borders are drawn not to protect life, but to project power. Resources are extracted to sustain the center. The distributed life God designed gives way to centralized control.

What is most striking is that Scripture does not interrupt this process immediately. There is no thunderous judgment, no dramatic collapse. Empire is allowed to develop. Its consequences will be revealed over time. The text simply names what has happened: the city has become a kingdom.

This restraint is important. It reminds the reader that empire is not evil because it is dramatic or oppressive in every moment, but because it relocates trust. Authority that should be derivative becomes ultimate. Power that should serve begins to rule. What was meant to steward creation now reorganizes it according to its own needs.

In this way, empire represents the maturation of rebellion. Where the city sought safety, the kingdom seeks control. Where the city resisted dispersion, the kingdom enforces unity. Where Babel feared being scattered, empire ensures that scattering cannot occur without permission.

Genesis presents this transformation without commentary because it does not need explanation. The pattern will repeat itself so consistently throughout history that recognition becomes inevitable. From this point forward, human civilization will be shaped by kingdoms and empires—each promising order, permanence, and greatness, each exacting a cost borne by people and land alike.

The city has become a kingdom. And with that transformation, rebellion acquires scale.

Expansion as Necessity, Not Accident

Once authority is centralized, expansion ceases to be a choice and becomes a requirement. A kingdom cannot remain static without undermining the very structures that hold it together. Power concentrated at a center generates demands that exceed the resources of that center alone. Administration, enforcement, supply, and security all require continual extension. Empire expands not first because it desires to conquer, but because it must sustain itself.

The city gathers people; the kingdom organizes them; the empire must feed, defend, and control them. Density creates dependence. Dependence creates vulnerability. Vulnerability demands protection, and protection requires reach. Borders extend not merely to gain territory, but to stabilize the core. What begins as consolidation inevitably presses outward.

Genesis reflects this logic with restraint. Nimrod's kingdom begins at Babel, but it does not remain there. Authority moves into Assyria. New cities are founded.

Control spreads along routes of trade, agriculture, and communication. Expansion follows the lines of necessity rather than ambition alone. The empire does not ask whether it should grow; it asks whether it can afford not to.

This outward movement reshapes both people and land. Populations are relocated. Resources are extracted. Local rhythms are subordinated to imperial needs. The farther authority extends, the more impersonal it becomes. Decisions made at the center affect lives at the margins, often without regard for place, season, or consequence. Stewardship gives way to management; care gives way to calculation.

Expansion also hardens power. As distance increases, authority must rely less on relationship and more on force. Law replaces trust. Coercion replaces consent. The ruler becomes increasingly isolated, surrounded by systems designed to maintain control rather than truth. The empire grows outward even as it grows inwardly brittle.

Creation bears this weight alongside humanity. Land is pressed beyond rest. Agriculture shifts from sustenance to surplus. Forests, fields, and waters are reorganized to serve scale rather than balance. The earth is not destroyed, but strained—made to serve purposes foreign to its design. The groaning of creation intensifies as the empire extends its reach.

What makes expansion particularly dangerous is that it disguises necessity as destiny. Growth is framed as progress. Control is framed as order. Resistance is framed as chaos. Empire convinces itself that its spread is not merely required, but justified. In doing so, it becomes blind to the costs it imposes on both people and land.

Genesis does not pause to condemn this process explicitly, because it does not need to. The pattern will repeat so reliably throughout history that recognition becomes inevitable. Wherever power is centralized and permanence is sought through control, expansion will follow. Empire is not a failure of restraint alone; it is the natural outcome of authority detached from submission to God.

By the time empire reaches maturity, it can no longer imagine life without growth. To stop expanding would be to unravel. To slow would be to weaken. And so the cycle continues—outward movement driven not by vision, but by necessity. What began as an attempt to stabilize life now destabilizes the world around it.

Expansion is not empire's excess. It is its logic.

Order Without Submission

Empire does not present itself as chaos, but as order. Its appeal lies precisely in its ability to organize life, suppress disorder, and impose coherence on a fractured world. Roads are built. Laws are enforced. Borders are secured. Violence is regulated rather than unleashed. To a world weary of instability, empire offers predictability.

But this order is achieved without submission to God.

The distinction matters. Biblical order flows from alignment with God's will; imperial order flows from control. One arises from trust, the other from management. One respects limits; the other overrides them. Empire does not ask whether life is rightly ordered, but whether it is efficiently governed.

This is why empire often appears successful. It produces visible results. It standardizes behavior. It creates systems capable of sustaining large populations. Yet beneath this surface coherence lies a deeper dislocation. Order is no longer oriented toward righteousness, but toward the preservation of power. Stability becomes an end in itself.

In such a system, obedience replaces faith. People comply not because they trust, but because they are compelled. Law substitutes for conscience. Authority substitutes for accountability. What matters is not whether life is lived rightly, but whether it is lived acceptably within the system. Order is maintained, but truth is negotiable.

This form of order reshapes the human heart. Dependence shifts subtly but decisively. Where people once looked to God for provision and justice, they now look to the state. Security is no longer received as a gift, but demanded as a right. Gratitude gives way to expectation. Authority becomes the mediator of life's coherence.

Order without submission also alters the moral imagination. Because empire can suppress visible disorder, it convinces itself that it has addressed the problem of evil. Violence is controlled, crime is punished, dissent is managed. Yet the deeper rebellion of the heart remains untouched. Empire does not redeem; it regulates.

Creation, too, is folded into this logic. The natural world is ordered not according to its rhythms, but according to imperial need. Land is surveyed, categorized, and exploited. Seasons are pressured. Resources are consumed to sustain scale. What was meant to be stewarded becomes something to be administered.

This is the quiet danger of imperial order. It replaces chaos with control, but never asks whether control itself has become a substitute for trust. The world appears stable, yet it is held together by force rather than faith. Peace is maintained, but it is a managed peace—fragile, conditional, and dependent upon continued dominance.

Genesis does not accuse empire of disorder; it exposes a deeper failure. Order without submission cannot endure because it is untethered from the source of true order. The more empire relies on its own structures, the more it must reinforce them. What begins as governance becomes compulsion. What begins as stability becomes rigidity.

By the time empire reaches its full expression, it has achieved what it set out to do: it has replaced dependence on God with dependence on power. Life continues, but it is no longer oriented upward. Order remains, but submission has been displaced.

At that point, only one question remains unanswered: by what right does this order rule absolutely?

Creation Under Domination

As empire consolidates power and expands its reach, the effects are not confined to governance or social order. The created world itself is drawn into the logic of domination. Land, labor, and life are no longer stewarded locally, but reorganized to serve centralized authority. What was once received as a gift becomes something to be measured, administered, and exploited.

Under empire, creation is no longer encountered as a partner in stewardship, but as a resource. Fields are assessed for yield rather than rest. Forests are valued for timber rather than habitat. Rivers are redirected, roads cut through terrain, and landscapes reshaped to serve scale and efficiency. The earth is pressed into service for purposes foreign to its design. Dominion becomes domination.

This transformation does not occur through overt hostility toward creation, but through abstraction. Distance grows between decision and consequence. Those who rule no longer live where the land is worked. Policies are crafted far from the soil they affect. Extraction becomes easier when suffering is unseen. Creation groans not because it is hated, but because it is managed from afar.

Empire also alters humanity's relationship to labor. Work ceases to be primarily vocational or familial and becomes instrumental. People are organized as units of productivity, relocated according to need, and valued for output rather than presence. The rhythms that once governed life—season, rest, inheritance— are subordinated to imperial demand. Time itself is reorganized.

As scale increases, resilience decreases. Local knowledge is displaced by centralized control. What once could adapt slowly now must conform quickly. Failure spreads farther and faster. Famine, displacement, and environmental degradation are no longer isolated tragedies, but systemic outcomes. The cost of maintaining order is transferred outward—to the margins, to the land, to generations not yet born.

This domination also intensifies the groaning already present in creation. The earth bears not only the weight of human sin, but the compounded strain of human systems designed without regard for limits. Dominion, severed from submission to God, becomes a burden rather than care. The mandate to rule the earth is inverted into the demand that the earth sustain rule.

Genesis does not need to linger here. The pattern will become unmistakable across history. Wherever empire rises, creation is reorganized to serve it. The world becomes less hospitable not through divine curse alone, but through cumulative pressure. What God designed to flourish under stewardship strains under domination.

Nimrod as Pattern, Not Person

Genesis gives us remarkably little detail about Nimrod's life, and that restraint is intentional. We are not told how he ruled, how long he lived, or how his reign ended. Scripture offers no moral evaluation, no narrative rise or fall. Instead, Nimrod is introduced, situated, and then allowed to recede into the background. What matters is not the man himself, but what he represents.

Nimrod stands in Scripture not as a character to be analyzed, but as a pattern to be recognized. He is the first embodiment of a form of power that will appear again and again wherever human rebellion seeks permanence through control. His significance lies not in his personality, but in the structure he inaugurates.

This is why Genesis describes Nimrod in terms of function rather than story. He is "a mighty one in the earth," a ruler whose authority reshapes human life beyond his immediate presence. The cities associated with him endure. The kingdoms he establishes persist. Power outlives the person who first consolidates it. Empire is always larger than its founder.

By presenting Nimrod this way, Scripture teaches the reader how to understand history. The danger is not merely charismatic leaders or unusually forceful individuals. The danger is the recurring logic that produces them. When fear seeks stability, consolidation seeks permanence, and authority seeks legitimacy, a Nimrod figure will emerge. The name changes. The pattern remains.

This helps explain why the biblical story does not treat empire as an anomaly. From Genesis onward, kingdoms rise with predictable regularity. Each presents itself as necessary. Each claims to impose order. Each promises security. And each relies on the same structural commitments: centralized power, enforced unity, managed order, and expanding control.

Nimrod, then, is not an ancient curiosity. He is the prototype. He shows what happens when rebellion is no longer merely individual or collective, but institutional. What Cain built defensively and Babel attempted collectively, Nimrod organizes systematically. Rebellion gains endurance by becoming normal.

Understanding Nimrod as a pattern rather than a person also clarifies why Scripture resists locating evil solely in individual rulers. Kings can be wicked or just, strong or weak, but the structure they inherit exerts pressure regardless of character. Even well-intentioned rulers find themselves compelled to preserve systems that demand control, expansion, and enforcement. The problem is not simply who rules, but how rule itself has been conceived.

This perspective guards against both naïveté and cynicism. It prevents us from imagining that the right leader will redeem the structure, or that removing a single tyrant will heal the world. Empire does not depend on a villain; it depends on a logic that rewards consolidation and punishes restraint.

Genesis names Nimrod briefly and then moves on because the story does not end with him. It continues wherever power becomes centralized, wherever cities become kingdoms, and wherever order is maintained without submission to God. Nimrod is not remembered because he was unique, but because he was first.

From this point forward, Scripture will trace the consequences of this pattern repeatedly. Empires will rise and fall, each claiming legitimacy, each shaping life through control. The names will differ, but the structure will be familiar. The world will continue to groan beneath systems that promise order while quietly displacing trust.

Nimrod fades from the narrative, but his pattern does not. It becomes one of the defining features of human history—awaiting not reform, but resolution.

Empire Requires Worship

Empire cannot sustain itself by force alone. Authority that governs vast populations, diverse cultures, and extended territories must eventually answer a deeper question than obedience: legitimacy. Why this ruler? Why this order? Why should loyalty be absolute? Law can regulate behavior, and force can suppress resistance, but neither can secure the heart. Power, once centralized and expanded, must justify itself.

At this point, empire turns toward the sacred.

This movement is not accidental, nor is it uniquely Roman. It is the logical outcome of authority that has displaced submission to God. When power no longer derives its legitimacy from divine order, it must generate its own. The simplest and most enduring solution is sacralization. The ruler becomes more than an administrator. He becomes necessary. More than necessary, he becomes ultimate.

Worship enters not because emperors are inherently divine, but because divinity stabilizes power. A ruler who governs by force alone must constantly assert control. A ruler who is revered governs through allegiance. When authority is clothed in sacred meaning, obedience becomes more than compliance —it becomes devotion. Dissent becomes more than disobedience—it becomes impiety.

This is why empire consistently drifts toward worship. The personalization of power creates a vacuum that only the sacred can fill. Once the ruler embodies authority, expansion demands loyalty, and order depends on coherence, the ruler must stand above critique. To challenge him is to threaten stability itself. Divinity provides the necessary insulation.

Genesis does not narrate this development in detail, but it anticipates it. Nimrod stands at the threshold of this transformation. He is not described as divine, but he inaugurates a structure that cannot endure without divinization. Once authority is centralized, expanded, and detached from submission to God, worship is no longer optional. It is required.

This worship need not be overt at first. It often begins symbolically—through titles, images, rituals, and festivals. The ruler is praised as savior, protector, benefactor. Gratitude hardens into reverence. Reverence matures into devotion. Over time, the line between loyalty and worship dissolves. What began as honor becomes obligation.

Creation itself is folded into this system. Land and people alike are claimed as belonging to the ruler. Time is marked by imperial calendars. Space is defined by imperial presence. Even the heavens are enlisted, as rulers associate themselves with stars, destiny, and cosmic order. The empire does not merely rule the world; it interprets it.

At this stage, empire has achieved its final form. Order is complete, expansion is sustained, and authority is sacralized. Humanity no longer merely replaces God in practice; it replaces Him symbolically. The ruler stands where God should stand, mediating meaning, security, and identity.

This is the final expression of rebellion—not chaos, but counterfeit order. Not lawlessness, but law enthroned. Not the absence of worship, but misdirected worship. Humanity does not cease to be religious; it simply redirects its devotion toward power that promises what only God can give.

The tragedy is not that empire worships rulers, but that it *must.* Having displaced submission to God, it cannot survive without replacing Him. The emperor becomes a god not because he seeks blasphemy, but because empire cannot endure without an ultimate object of trust.

Genesis leaves this reality unresolved, not because it is incomplete, but because its resolution lies beyond empire itself. The story will move forward, tracing kingdoms and rulers who rise and fall under this same logic. The world will continue to groan beneath structures that promise order while demanding worship.

The question that remains is not whether empire will arise, but whether there is another kind of kingdom— one that rules without domination, orders without control, and receives worship without coercion.

Summary

Genesis traces the maturation of rebellion with deliberate restraint. What begins as fear seeking refuge becomes permanence sought through structure. The city answers vulnerability with proximity. The kingdom organizes life through centralized authority. Empire extends control outward, reshaping people, land, and meaning itself. Each step appears reasonable, even necessary, yet each moves further from submission to God.

Nimrod stands not as an isolated ruler, but as the embodiment of a pattern. Power becomes personal, expansion becomes unavoidable, and order is achieved without righteousness. What begins as management of life becomes domination over it. Creation itself is drawn into the system, pressed beyond its design to sustain scale and control. The earth groans—not only under human sin, but under human systems built to replace trust with force.

Empire's final necessity is worship. Authority that has displaced God cannot endure without sacralizing itself. The ruler becomes the mediator of order, the guarantor of stability, and ultimately the object of devotion. Rebellion reaches its most complete form not in chaos, but in counterfeit order—law enthroned, power justified, worship redirected.

Genesis offers no dramatic collapse at this point. Empire is allowed to stand. The pattern is named and left unresolved. Humanity has succeeded in building a world that functions without submission to God, yet the cost is borne by both people and land. The world continues, but it does not heal. It groans.

At this stage of the biblical story, the problem is fully exposed. Creation is subjected to futility—not because it is evil, but because it is bound to humanity's rebellion. Sin does not remain personal; it becomes generational. It reshapes environments, systems, and expectations. The earth bears the compounded weight of human autonomy across time.

Yet Scripture does not end with empire.

The groaning of creation is not merely the sound of decay; it is the sound of longing. What has been subjected is not abandoned. What has been distorted is not beyond redemption. The story must now move beyond diagnosis toward promise—not through another human structure, but through divine intervention.

The final chapter will trace this hope. From Paul's declaration that creation itself waits for liberation, to John's vision of a city that descends rather than rises, Scripture reveals a different kind of order—one that restores rather than dominates. Eden is not erased, but expanded. What was lost through rebellion is secured through redemption.

The world that groans will become the world made new.

The World Made New

6

The World That Groans / The World Made New

Creation Subjected to Futility

By the time the biblical witness reaches its later testimony, the problem is no longer confined to individual sin or isolated acts of rebellion. What began as a human choice has become a condition shared by the world itself. Creation bears the consequences of humanity's autonomy not as an observer, but as a participant bound to human vocation. The earth does not merely host the story of sin; it carries it.

Paul gives language to this reality with striking clarity. Creation, he says, was "subjected to futility"—not willingly, not by its own rebellion, but because it was bound to humanity's choice. This statement does not

135

introduce a new idea; it names what Genesis has been showing all along. From the moment humanity grasped autonomy, the ground itself entered into the consequences of that decision. The curse was not arbitrary. It was relational. Humanity's role as steward meant that its rebellion could not remain private.

The futility Paul describes is not purposelessness, but frustration. Creation continues to function, to produce, to sustain life—but never without resistance. The ground yields, yet with thorns. The waters sustain, yet overwhelm. The world provides, yet with fragility. Life persists, but it no longer aligns effortlessly with human flourishing. What once cooperated now strains.

Genesis traces this strain carefully. The ground is cursed in Adam. Violence fills the earth in Cain's line. The Flood releases the waters once restrained. Afterward, creation is reorganized under human systems that intensify its burden. Empire presses land and labor into service. Yet at no point is creation portrayed as rebelling against God. Scripture consistently presents the created order as obedient— declaring God's glory, responding to His word, and bearing witness to His power. The heavens still proclaim. The seasons still turn. The earth continues to give testimony to its Maker.

Creation groans, then, not as a defiant actor, but as a faithful witness placed under strain. It suffers not because it has rejected God, but because it has been bound to humanity's misrule. The world bears a weight it was never designed to carry, even as it continues to do what it was created to do. Its groaning is not protest against God, but lament under human autonomy. This futility is not the result of divine neglect. Paul is explicit: creation was subjected "in hope." God binds the world's future to redemption rather than abandonment. The curse is not a verdict of annihilation, but a condition awaiting resolution. Creation's groaning is not despairing noise; it is expectant tension. The world strains toward a future it cannot yet reach.

This perspective reframes suffering in the natural world. Decay, disaster, and instability are not signs that creation has become hostile to God, but that it remains bound to humanity's unfinished story. The earth is not morally corrupt, but relationally burdened. It waits for humanity to become what it was created to be, because only then can creation be what it was meant to be.

Paul's language also resists sentimental readings. Creation does not groan because it longs to escape existence, but because it longs for liberation. The problem is not embodiment, matter, or physicality. The problem is disorder without redemption. Creation yearns not for dissolution, but for restoration.

This is why futility and hope are held together so tightly. The present order is not final, but neither is it meaningless. God has not abandoned His world, nor has He accelerated its destruction. He has subjected it to a condition that preserves life while refusing to allow rebellion to feel permanent. Futility prevents autonomy from becoming eternal.

In this way, creation becomes a witness. Its groaning testifies that the world is not as it should be, but also that it is not beyond healing. Every strain, every fracture, every resistance reminds humanity that it was not created to rule alone. Creation's frustration echoes God's own grief—not as accusation, but as invitation.

The world groans because it is waiting. And it waits not for escape from humanity, but for humanity's redemption.

Generational and Environmental Consequences of Sin

Sin does not end with the individual act that introduces it. It accumulates. What begins as personal rebellion becomes an inherited condition, embedded not only in human behavior but in the environments shaped by it. Scripture consistently portrays sin as generational—not merely because children imitate parents, but because the consequences of human autonomy are carried forward in land, systems, and memory.

Genesis makes this progression visible early. Adam's choice alters the ground his children will till. Cain's violence introduces a pattern that fills the earth. The Flood restrains corruption but does not erase its residue. Afterward, humanity reorganizes life through cities, kingdoms, and empires that intensify strain rather than heal it. Each generation inherits not a neutral world, but one already shaped by the choices of those who came before.

This inheritance is not moral guilt transferred mechanically, but burden transferred structurally. Fields exhausted by misuse do not recover quickly. Waters polluted by neglect do not cleanse themselves overnight. Systems built for control rather than care do not dissolve when their founders die. The earth retains the imprint of rebellion long after the rebels are gone.

Scripture acknowledges this reality without embarrassment. God warns that the consequences of sin reach "to the third and fourth generation," not as arbitrary punishment, but as lived reality. Patterns established in one generation shape the possibilities of the next. Freedom is constrained by what has already been done to people and land alike.

Environmental consequence is one expression of this truth. The earth responds faithfully to how it is treated. When land is stewarded with restraint, it flourishes. When it is pressed for dominance, it resists. Famine, instability, and ecological breakdown are not merely natural phenomena; they are often the cumulative result of long-term misrule. Creation does not forget. It remembers through diminished yield, increased fragility, and amplified vulnerability.

Yet Scripture refuses to locate blame in creation itself. The land does not curse humanity. It reflects humanity. It gives back what it has been asked to bear. When sin compounds across generations, creation becomes the archive of that history. The groaning grows louder not because creation grows more hostile, but because the burden has grown heavier.

This generational dimension also explains why reform alone cannot heal the world. Even sincere repentance occurs within inherited conditions. People seek to live faithfully on ground already strained, within systems already bent. Good intentions do not immediately reverse accumulated damage. Healing requires time, patience, and intervention beyond human capacity.

Here again, Romans 8 provides clarity. Creation waits not merely for better stewardship, but for liberation. The problem is not simply that humans have ruled poorly, but that they cannot, on their own, undo the weight of what has already been done. Sin's consequences outlast sin's moment. The world groans under a history it did not choose.

And yet, hope remains bound to this very reality. Because creation has borne the cost of human rebellion, it will also share in humanity's redemption. The same generational logic that compounds damage becomes the pathway through which restoration spreads. Redemption, like sin, is not merely individual. It is cosmic.

The earth waits, then, not for abandonment, but for renewal. Its groaning testifies that the story is unfinished—and that the One who subjected it in hope has not forgotten what it has borne.

Managing Failure and Prophesying Victory

The Old Testament unfolds in the shadow of a problem it does not pretend to solve. Creation groans. Sin compounds. Human systems bend toward domination. Within this reality, God does not immediately erase the damage or reset the world again. Instead, He works within history to restrain collapse and preserve hope. The story that follows is not one of steady improvement, but of managed failure.

This management is not resignation. It is mercy.

From the moment humanity leaves Eden, God engages a world that cannot be healed all at once. Violence must be restrained. Justice must be approximated. Worship must be redirected. The Law is given not because it can restore creation, but because it can limit destruction. It draws boundaries around behavior that would otherwise accelerate decay. It names sin, curbs excess, and preserves the possibility of life together.

Kings arise not as ideal rulers, but as concessions to human demand. Scripture does not hide their inadequacy. Even the best of them rule imperfectly; most fail openly. Yet kingship functions as containment. Authority is localized. Violence is regulated. Chaos is delayed. The system creaks under its own weight, but it holds long enough for promise to endure.

Sacrifice operates in the same way. It does not eliminate sin; it acknowledges it. Blood is shed not to perfect the worshiper, but to maintain relationship. The system bears witness to its own insufficiency. Again and again, it declares that something more is required. The very repetition of sacrifice is a confession that the wound remains open.

The prophets enter this managed failure not as optimists, but as truth-tellers. They do not celebrate the system; they expose it. They name injustice, condemn domination, and remind Israel that survival is not the same as faithfulness. Yet even their words are acts of mercy. Judgment is announced not to destroy hope, but to sever illusion. God will not allow His people to mistake restraint for redemption.

Exile becomes the clearest expression of this pattern. It is not the abandonment of God's people, but the collapse of their false securities. Land, temple, and throne are stripped away, revealing that none of them were ultimate. Yet even in exile, promise remains. Failure is managed, not erased. The story continues.

Throughout this history, the Old Testament refuses to claim that the present order is sufficient. It preserves life, restrains evil, and maintains covenant—but it does not heal creation. The earth still groans. Generational wounds persist. Human hearts remain bent. Management prevents the worst outcomes, but it cannot produce the best.

And this is precisely the point. The Old Testament prepares the world not by fixing it, but by preventing despair. It keeps the future open. It refuses to let rebellion become final. In doing so, it creates space for something entirely new—not another system of restraint, but the arrival of restoration itself.

Failure is managed so that victory can be promised.

The Blueprint of Renewal: Foundation Before Fulfillment

The New Testament does not begin by dismantling the groaning world. It begins by laying a foundation within it. This is a crucial distinction. God does not announce immediate replacement, but intentional renovation. What has been managed through restraint will now be addressed through renewal—but renewal proceeds according to design, not haste.

This is why the gospel does not read like a revolution manifesto. There is no sudden collapse of empire, no immediate healing of creation, no instant reversal of futility. Instead, Christ appears quietly, embodying a different kind of authority, inaugurating a kingdom that does not seize space but transforms it. The work begins at the deepest level, where foundations are laid.

Peter provides the language for this moment. Christ is the living stone, chosen by God and rejected by builders, set in place as the cornerstone. A cornerstone does not complete a structure; it determines its alignment. Everything that follows depends on its placement. Without it, construction is impossible. With it, fulfillment becomes certain, even if incomplete.

John, writing from the other end of the story, shows the finished work. He does not describe a repaired empire or a perfected human system, but a city that descends from God, radiant and secure. Between Peter's foundation and John's vision lies the long work of renovation—the slow, costly transformation of a world that still groans.

This sequence matters. Fulfillment without foundation would be collapse. Restoration without alignment would reproduce the old order in new form. God does not replace domination with chaos, nor does He sanctify control. He rebuilds from the ground up, beginning with obedience rather than power, faithfulness rather than force.

The blueprint of renewal also explains why the old order is allowed to persist for a time. Foundations are laid quietly. Load-bearing structures are reinforced. What cannot survive the renovation is exposed and removed. What can be redeemed is incorporated. The process is not visible to every observer, but it is decisive.

This is why the New Testament speaks so often in architectural terms. The household of God is being built. Living stones are fitted together. The Spirit dwells within a structure still under construction. These metaphors are not incidental. They remind the reader that the work underway is neither cosmetic nor symbolic. It is structural.

The delay between foundation and fulfillment is not absence; it is mercy. It allows the renovation to spread without coercion. It prevents the new creation from becoming another imposed order. God does not conquer the world into submission; He renews it into alignment.

The blueprint also guards against despair. Because the foundation is already laid, the outcome is not in doubt. The groaning continues, but it does so beneath a structure that will not fail. What remains unfinished is not uncertain. Fulfillment waits, but it does not waver.

The New Testament, then, does not announce the end of the world that groans. It announces the beginning of the world made new. The work has started where it must start—at the foundation—so that when fulfillment comes, it will endure.

The Second Adam and the Restoration of Dominion

At the heart of the world's renewal stands a Man. Scripture does not answer the failure of dominion with a new system, nor the groaning of creation with another structure of power. It answers both with the Second Adam. Where the first Adam grasped autonomy and fractured humanity's vocation, Christ receives authority and restores it.

This contrast is deliberate and decisive. The first Adam sought life apart from submission, and in doing so, lost dominion. The ground resisted. Creation strained. Authority gave way to fear, then to domination. The Second Adam moves in the opposite direction. He does not seize authority; it is given to Him. He does not rule through force; He reigns through obedience. Dominion is not reclaimed by control, but by faithfulness.

Jesus enters a world fully shaped by empire. Power is centralized. Authority is sacralized. Order is enforced. Yet He refuses every familiar path to rule. He declines the temptation to grasp the kingdoms of the world. He rejects violence as a means of authority. He embodies a kingship that operates without domination. In doing so, He exposes the old order not as ultimate, but as temporary.

The restoration of dominion begins not with command, but with submission. Christ submits to the Father's will, even unto death. This obedience does not weaken His authority; it establishes it. Where Adam's disobedience subjected creation to futility, Christ's obedience opens the path to liberation. Dominion is restored not by overcoming creation, but by reconciling it.

Paul names this reversal explicitly. As death came through one man, so life comes through another. The Second Adam does not merely undo Adam's failure;

He exceeds it. He does not return humanity to Eden's vulnerability, but carries it toward secured glory. Resurrection marks the turning point. Creation's future is bound not to decay, but to transformed life.

This restored dominion is already operative, though not yet complete. Christ reigns, yet the world still groans. Authority has been redefined, but not universally recognized. The renovation is underway, but the scaffolding remains. Dominion has been reclaimed at the foundation, even as its full expression awaits fulfillment.

Importantly, Christ's dominion does not mirror empire in sanctified form. It does not centralize power for control, nor does it require worship to sustain authority. Worship flows freely because His reign gives life rather than demands it. Where empire required worship to stabilize itself, Christ receives worship as the natural response to restoration.

Under the Second Adam, creation is no longer managed into submission but invited into renewal. The earth is not pressed for productivity but promised freedom. Humanity's calling as steward is recovered —not as domination, but as shared participation in God's purposes. The groaning of creation begins to shift in tone, from despair toward hope.

This is why the New Testament speaks of Christ as firstfruits. His resurrection is not an isolated miracle, but the beginning of a pattern. What has happened in Him will happen in creation. The restoration of dominion is not theoretical; it has already entered history.

The old order of domination is passing away, not because it has been overthrown by greater force, but because it has been rendered obsolete. Authority no longer belongs to those who seize it. It belongs to the One who received it faithfully.

In the Second Adam, dominion is reclaimed, creation is reoriented, and the future is secured. The world still groans—but now it groans in hope.

The New Jerusalem: Eden Regained, Expanded, and Secured

The biblical story does not end with escape from the world that groans. It ends with the renewal of that world. John's vision in Revelation does not describe humanity ascending out of creation, but God descending into it. What empire sought to build upward in Babel, God brings down in grace. The final city is not the product of human ambition; it is the gift of divine presence.

The New Jerusalem descends from God, prepared, radiant, and secure. This movement is decisive. The city of the future does not rise through conquest or consolidation. It arrives whole, complete, and ordered by righteousness. Authority does not originate within its walls; it proceeds from the throne of God and of the Lamb. Power is no longer centralized for control, but shared as life.

This city fulfills what Eden promised but could not secure. Eden was good, but vulnerable. Its boundaries were guarded. Its access could be lost. The New Jerusalem is not merely a restored garden; it is a consummated dwelling. What was once local becomes global. What was once fragile becomes permanent. The tree of life returns—not hidden, not protected by cherubim, but freely accessible. Healing flows outward rather than being withheld.

The contrast with empire could not be sharper. Babel built to make a name; the New Jerusalem bears God's name. Empire guarded its gates; this city's gates stand open. Empire required enforced unity; the nations walk freely in the light. Diversity is not erased, but redeemed. Glory is brought in, not extracted. Order exists without domination. Authority serves life rather than demanding sacrifice.

Most striking is what is absent. There is no temple, because God dwells fully with His people. There is no sea of chaos, because disorder has been undone. There is no curse, because futility has reached its end. Creation's groaning gives way to rest—not the rest of inactivity, but of alignment. Life finally moves in harmony with God's purposes.

This vision does not abandon the material world. It completes it. Bodies are raised. Creation is healed. Time continues, but without decay. Humanity's vocation is not revoked, but fulfilled. Dominion is no longer exercised through control, but through communion. The steward finally becomes what he was created to be.

The New Jerusalem also resolves the problem of power. There is a throne—but it is not occupied by one who seized authority. The Lamb reigns because He was slain. His authority is cruciform, not coercive. Worship is not demanded to stabilize His rule; it flows naturally because His reign restores life. The emperor-as-god is finally answered—not by replacement, but by exposure. True authority never required domination.

Here, the long arc of Scripture finds its rest. The world subjected to futility is liberated. The systems that managed failure are no longer needed. The blueprint laid in Christ is fully realized. What was begun quietly is completed gloriously. Eden is not simply regained; it is expanded and secured forever.

The story that began with humanity grasping autonomy ends with humanity dwelling in trust. God is with His people. Creation is whole. The groaning ceases—not because creation is silenced, but because it is satisfied.

The World Made New

This is not the end of the world.

It is the world, at last, made new.

"Cursed Is the Ground for Thy Sake": Judgment, Consequence, and the Groaning of Creation (Genesis 3:17)

Few phrases in Scripture have shaped the Christian imagination more powerfully—or more imprecisely—than God's words to Adam in Genesis 3:17: "cursed is the ground for thy sake." These words stand at the crossroads of creation, sin, judgment, and hope. How they are understood will determine whether the groaning of the world is interpreted as divine hostility, arbitrary punishment, or moral consequence.

Because this book builds its argument upon the relationship between human autonomy and creation's resistance, this passage deserves careful, unhurried attention.

Why This Phrase Matters

Genesis 3 does not merely explain that the world is broken; it explains why it is broken and how God responds to that breakage. The curse pronounced upon the ground is not an incidental detail. It is the first moment in Scripture where creation itself is directly affected by human rebellion. From this point forward, the soil will resist, labor will strain, and death will loom—not because creation has turned against God, but because humanity has fractured its role within creation.

If this curse is understood primarily as retaliatory anger, then the groaning of creation becomes evidence of divine hostility. If it is understood as moral consequence, then the groaning becomes evidence of divine faithfulness—to truth, to order, and ultimately to redemption.

What the Text Actually Says

The Hebrew construction translated "for thy sake" carries a range of meaning that includes on account of, because of, and with reference to. Importantly, it does not require the sense of vengeance or emotional retaliation. God does not say, "I curse the ground to harm you," nor does He curse Adam himself. Instead, He identifies the sphere in which Adam's choice will now be experienced.

The ground is cursed because of Adam—not as an act of spite, but as a consequence of role reversal. Humanity was created from the ground and appointed as its steward. When the steward rejects trust in God and claims autonomy, the relationship between humanity and creation cannot remain harmonious. The ground resists not because God delights in struggle, but because autonomy has placed humanity at odds with the very order it was meant to serve.

Curse as Moral Necessity, Not Caprice

The curse is not the introduction of evil into creation; it is the exposure of what life looks like when trust is severed. Adam desired to know good and evil apart from God. God grants that desire—not by inventing wickedness, but by allowing humanity to experience life governed by its own will rather than God's.

In this sense, the curse is permissive rather than inventive. God does not design futility; He permits humanity to encounter it. Creation's resistance is not punishment layered on top of rebellion; it is rebellion's natural outworking within a world ordered toward God.

This distinction matters. A curse rooted in caprice would undermine God's goodness. A curse rooted in moral necessity preserves it. God remains righteous, faithful, and unchanging—not reacting emotionally to sin, but responding truthfully to what humanity has chosen.

Judgment That Restrains, Not Destroys

Even here, mercy is evident. The ground is cursed, but it still yields. Labor is difficult, but not impossible. Life is limited, but not immediately extinguished. The curse restrains humanity from eternalizing rebellion. Immortality in autonomy would freeze evil forever. By introducing resistance, toil, and death, God preserves the possibility of repentance and redemption.

This restraint anticipates later Scripture. Paul's language in Romans 8—that creation was "subjected to futility, not willingly"—echoes Genesis 3. Creation groans not in rebellion against God, but under the burden of humanity's sin, awaiting restoration. The curse is not the final word; it is a temporary condition within a redemptive arc.

Why This Reading Matters for the Whole Book

Understanding Genesis 3:17 as consequence rather than retaliation allows the rest of Scripture to unfold coherently. Cain's violence, the rise of cities, the spread of domination, the Flood, empire, and even exile all follow the same pattern: humanity insisting on autonomy, and God allowing that insistence to run its course within limits.

Most importantly, this reading preserves hope. If creation's groaning were the product of divine hostility, redemption would require God to change His mind. But if groaning is the result of humanity's rebellion within a faithful creation order, then redemption consists not in undoing God's judgment, but in restoring humanity's place within God's design.

Appendix

The ground was cursed because of Adam—but it was never abandoned. From that soil would come altars, sacrifices, covenants, and ultimately a cross planted in cursed earth. The God who allowed the ground to resist is the same God who promised that one day creation itself would be set free.

The curse explains why the world groans.

The gospel explains why it will not groan forever.

FIREPROOF
COMMENTARIES

Fireproof Commentaries

Deep Scripture. Clear Explanation. Practical Faith.

Fireproof Commentaries is a Bible study series crafted for pastors, teachers, and thoughtful Christians who refuse to settle for shallow interpretation or surface-level application. Each volume enters the biblical text with rigorous care, honoring the original context and the theological contours of Scripture, while always pointing readers to the sufficiency of Christ.

This series is not a collection of devotional reflections, nor is it a technical academic commentary. Instead, Fireproof Commentaries bridges the gap between careful exegesis and real-world discipleship—helping readers understand what the Bible meant, why it matters now, and how it transforms our thinking and living.

Inside Each Volume:

- Faithful exposition grounded in the original languages and historical setting

- Theological insight that connects ancient revelation to contemporary life

- Pastoral clarity for preaching, teaching, and personal study

- Application that calls believers to deeper trust in Christ

Whether you are preparing a sermon, leading a small group, or cultivating your own walk with God, Fireproof Commentaries equips you to engage Scripture with confidence, clarity, and spiritual depth.

Read the Word. Understand the Word.

Live the Word.

www.ingramcontent.com/pod-product-compliance
Lightning Source LLC
Chambersburg PA
CBHW060426130626
46555CB00005B/2235